**CAMPAIGN
FOR
REAL ALE**

Edinburgh & South East Sc
Third Ed

GW01388481

Introduction

It is four years since the publication of the last edition of the Edinburgh & South East Scotland Real Ale Guide, the CAMRA guide to the availability of real ale in Edinburgh, the Lothians and the Borders. That edition listed over 300 pubs selling real ale and reported that, while the number of real ale outlets had remained fairly steady in the previous few years, the choice of ales available over that time had increased dramatically, due mainly to the appearance of micro breweries in many parts of Scotland.

Since then the number of micro breweries has not continued to increase at the previous rate - that would have been unsustainable - but it has held steady and almost all of the breweries existing in 2004 are still in business. The same is not true of the pubs alas, and there has been a slow but steady fall in the number of pubs in this area, especially in the remoter regions of the Borders. The usual pattern is that a pub is bought, deemed by the new owners to be unprofitable, closed and redeveloped for residential accommodation. The developer makes a tidy profit and you wonder how hard the new owners tried to make a go of the business. The loser is the local community which is deprived of its main hub.

Despite this, there are good real ale outlets to be found in most parts of South East Scotland and this guide lists details of over 305 pubs in Edinburgh, the Lothians and the Borders that serve real ale and/or real cider. It is intended to be a reference for the local real ale drinker, as well as a guide for visitors to the area. The information given on each pub varies in detail, but has been checked within six months of publication. With new pubs opening, and others changing their character on a regular basis, this guide is intended to be the latest in a long line of future editions. Every effort has been made to keep the price of the guide as low as possible so that the cost of up-grading to future revised editions will not be prohibitive.

The Pubs

All pubs, known to CAMRA in Edinburgh, West Lothian, Midlothian, East Lothian and the Scottish Borders, that serve real ale or cider are included in this guide, with the following exceptions: Pubs which serve a keg beer or cider through a handpump are excluded because CAMRA considers that this practice may mislead the public into thinking that these products are real; Pubs that apply gas, other than air, directly to their real ales are also excluded, as are a few outlets where entrance to the general public cannot be guaranteed.

How To Use This Guide

The pubs are divided into Borders and the Lothians. They are then listed alphabetically by town name and, within towns, by pub name. Maps are included in the centre of the guide. Pubs in Edinburgh have been given a grid reference which can be referred to the table of grid references and pub names, also in the centre of the guide. The address, post code and telephone number are listed and where necessary, additional directions are given. A guide to bus and rail transport is given for each pub, see the rear cover for more information. The website, traveline.org.uk, is a useful additional source of information.

The opening times given are intended to be those when alcohol is available. However a number of pubs open earlier for food and soft drinks.

The range of real ales and ciders constantly changes in many pubs. Those listed have appeared regularly on the bar in the six months or so prior to publication. The words "Guest Beer" or "Beer Range Varies" appear in many entries and this phrase covers the regularly changing real ales and ciders available in a pub. Many of the more interesting beers available in pubs appear on an occasional basis only. The symbols used after the beers indicate the method of dispense. A list of these is given inside the rear cover. Real ales and ciders dispensed using methods not approved by CAMRA are not listed.

Letter codes, listed inside the rear cover, describe the features and facilities of each pub.

What Is Real Ale?

Real ale is beer brewed with traditional ingredients, using traditional methods, and stored and served in the pub by traditional means. The most important difference between real ale and other types of beers is that the beer is still fermenting in the cask when it is delivered to the pub. The beer has to be left to settle in the pub cellar before being served and will produce its own condition, or sparkle. This is why you will often hear the beer being described as cask conditioned, or cask, ale. Real ale, cask conditioned ale and cask ale are the same thing. The casks are open to the atmosphere and no carbon dioxide or other gas is applied to make the beer fizzy.

In contrast, keg beers, now often sold as smooth or smoothflow beers, are dead when they arrive in the pub. They do not develop the same flavours and character found in real, living, ales as they are filtered and pasteurised at the brewery before being racked into containers and delivered to pubs. Once in the pub cellar carbon dioxide gas, or a mixture of carbon dioxide and nitrogen, is connected to the container to aid dispense of the beer and to give it the appearance of life. Smooth beer is dead beer!

What Is CAMRA?

The Campaign for Real Ale (CAMRA) has been described as the most successful consumer group in Europe. It is an independent, voluntary, consumer organisation with over 89,000 members who are lovers of traditional British beer. CAMRA promotes good-quality real ale and pubs, as well as acting as the consumer's champion in relation to the UK and European beer and drinks industry. It aims to:

- Protect and improve consumer rights;
- Promote quality, choice and value for money;
- Support the public house as a focus of community life;
- Campaign for greater appreciation of traditional beers, ciders and perries as part of our national heritage and culture;
- Seek improvements in all licensed premises and throughout the brewing industry.

Our aim is to ensure that British beer drinkers continue to have the chance to drink well kept real ale in as many pubs as possible around the country. We also campaign on many pub and beer related issues such as the right to be served a full pint of beer when that is what we have asked (and paid) for and the liberalisation of our licensing laws. Our views on beer related issues are sought and listened to by the governments in Edinburgh, London and Cardiff.

CAMRA also seeks to revive interest in traditional styles of beer that have disappeared or are facing declining sales. A prime example of this is the Scottish Light or 60/- ale. Like its English counterpart, mild, these beers are becoming increasingly hard to find. This is a great shame because they are usually quite flavoursome and low in alcohol which makes them ideal for lunchtime and other occasions when a refreshing pint is desired without any major after-effects.

The Local CAMRA Branch

The Campaign is organised on a regional basis, with numerous local groups or branches. The Edinburgh and South East Scotland Branch get together on a regular basis for meetings, socials and visits to pubs and breweries not only in the immediate locality but also throughout the UK. Although the activities inevitably involve drinking real ale at some point you do not have to be a gallon a day drinker to join in. Most members have to go to work the next day! One of the highlights of the year is the Scottish Traditional Beer Festival, held in the Assembly Rooms, George Street, Edinburgh on midsummer weekend. This is great fun to work at and an opportunity to sample some of the 100 plus beers brewed in Scotland as well.

If you enjoy drinking real ale and want to be part of one of the most successful consumer organisations in Europe then why not use the membership form, printed at the end of this guide, to join CAMRA.

The Breweries and their Beers

There is now a variety of breweries producing real ale in Scotland and many of their products are available on a regular basis throughout the area covered by this guide. Below there are brief details of the breweries and beers located in the branch area.

Belhaven Brewing Co.
Spott Road, Dunbar, EH42 1RS.   (01368) 862734
Long established brewery owned since 2005 by Greene King.
60/- (2.9%), 70/- (3.5%), Sandy Hunter's Ale (3.6%), 80/- Ale (4.2%), St Andrews Ale (4.9%).

Broughton Ales
Broughton, Biggar ML12 6HQ.   (01899) 830345
Founded in 1979, Broughton Ales has been brewing cask beers for more than 25 years but more than 60% of production is bottled for sale in Britain and export markets. Shop open Mon-Fri 8am-5pm.
Coulsons EPA (3.5%), The Reiver (3.8%), Bramling Cross (4.2%), Clipper IPA (4.2%), Merlin's Ale (4.2%), Exciseman's Ale (4.6%), Old Jock Ale (6.7%).

Caledonian Brewery
Slateford Road, Edinburgh EH11 1PH. (0131) 337 1286
Originally the Lorimer and Clark brewery, then bought by Vaux, Caledonian was formed by management buy-out in 1987. In 2004 the brewery site was sold to Scottish and Newcastle and in 2008, S&N bought the company outright. S&N has now been bought by Heineken.
Deuchars IPA (3.8%), 80 (4.1%), XPA (4.3%), Golden Promise (5.0%).

Stewart Brewing Ltd.
Unit 5, 42 Dryden Road Bilston Glen Industrial Estate EH20 9LZ. (0131) 440 2442
Established in 2004 and specialising in high-quality cask ales, all made from natural ingredients. Beer for home in can be purchased direct from the brewery for collection or delivery.
Pentland IPA (4.1%), Copper Cascade (4.2%), Edinburgh No 3 (4.3%), Stewart's 80/- (4.4%). Edinburgh Gold (4.8%),

Traquair House Brewery, Traquair House, Innerleithen EH44 6PW. (01896) 830323
Started in 1965. The 18th-century brew house is based in one of the wings of the 1,000-year-old Traquair House. All the beers are oak-fermented and 60 per cent of production is exported.
Bear Ale (ABV 5%), Traquair House Ale (ABV 7%), Jacobite Ale (ABV 8%)

Breweries currently not brewing (June 2008)

Fowler's Ales (Prestoungrange) Ltd, 227-229 High Street, Prestonpans, East Lothian EH32 9BE.
Opened in 2004 mainly to supply the adjacent Prestoungrange Gothenburg

McCowan's Brewhouse, 134 Dundee Street, Edinburgh EH11 1AF.
Opened originally in 1998 but has not brewed continuously since then.

Peelwalls Brewery, Peelwalls Farmhouse, Ayton, Eyemouth TD15 5Rl.
Started brewing beer in 2005.

The CAMRA National Inventory

As a consumer organisation, CAMRA has an interest in all matters related to pubs and pub culture, including pub history. As part of its efforts to protect and promote the heritage of the British pub, CAMRA has compiled an inventory of pub interiors which are of particular interest because they are examples of historical styles most of which have been destroyed by "modernisation". In practice, this means that they are much as they were at the end of the Second World War. The Inventory is divided into Part 1, which lists pubs whose interiors have remained largely unaltered since 1945 and also includes certain exceptional examples from the post-War era, and Part 2, which lists interiors which, although altered, have exceptional rooms or features of national historic importance. The list below gives all pubs in the Inventory which are in the branch area. Most of them serve real ale of course but there are one or two which don't. The Inventory is a statement about the architecture of a pub rather than what beer it sells.

Part 1	Edinburgh	Abbotsford, Rose Street.,
		Bennets Bar, Leven Street, Tollcross.
		H P Mather's Bar, Queensferry Street.
		Leslie's Bar, Ratcliffe Terrace.
		Oxford Bar, Young Street.
		Rutherford's Bar, Drummond Street.
	Selkirk	Town Arms, Market Place.

Part 2	Edinburgh	Café Royal, West Register Street.
		Kenilworth, Rose Street.
		Central Bar, Leith Walk, Leith.
	Oxton	Tower Hotel.
	Prestonpans	Prestoungrange Gothenburg.
	Tweedsmuir	Crook Inn.

And Finally

The Edinburgh and South East Scotland branch of CAMRA hope you will enjoy using this guide. Whilst every effort has been made to ensure the accuracy of the information shown, no responsibility can be accepted for errors, omissions or the changes that will inevitably occur during the currency of this edition. In particular, the presence or absence of a symbol cannot be taken as a guarantee that the facility is or is not available.

Craw Inn – CAMRA 2008 Borders Pub of the Year

Allanton

Allanton Inn

Allanton, TD11 3JZ

(01890) 818260

Bus: Wait's 260 - twice a day

12-2.00(not Mon & Tue), 6-10.30(not Sun & Mon; 11 Tue, Fri & Sat)

Beer Range (1) Varies[H] ☺

Welcoming Borders coaching inn. The front rooms are a restaurant serving a good varied menu (booking recommended). The back bar offers an interesting real ale or two.

AC OD (garden) ML (12-2 Sun) ME (6.30-8.30) BS (not Sun) DW

Ancrum

Cross Keys Inn

The Green, TD8 6XH

(01835) 830344

Bus: Most Jedburgh Buses

12-2.30(not Mon), 6-11(5-1am Fri); 12 - Midnight Sat; 12.30 - 11 Sun

Beer Range (3) Varies[H] ☺

Friendly village local with a bar that remains nearly untouched since 1908. It retains the pine panelling through into the gantry, has compact seating and tables made from old sewing machines. The spacious back lounge has been sympathetically refurbished and retains overhead tramlines from the former cellar. The good, varied menu is supplemented by daily specials. Free Wi-Fi access.

DA (thro' vennel) OD (tables at front & courtyard) ML (12-2.30) ME (6-9) BS CW (in lounge) DW (not where food served)

Auchencrow

Craw Inn

Auchencrow, TD14 5LS

(01890) 761253

12-2.30, 6-11(Midnight Fri); 12 - Midnight Sat; 12.30 - 11 Sun

Beer Range (2) Varies[H] ☺

Very friendly village inn, circa 1680. The beamed bar has bench seating at one end and wooden tables, chairs and a church pew by the log burning stove at the other. The two beers are usually from smaller breweries, and change frequently. The rear is a restaurant, which features special events during the course of the year. A beer festival is held in November. Awarded CAMRA Borders pub of the year 2008.

AC DA OD (rear patio & garden over road) ML (12.30-2) ME (6-9) BS CW

Bonchester Bridge

Horse & Hound

Bonchester Bridge, TD9 8JN

(01450) 860645

11.30-3, 5-11; 11.30 - Midnight Fri & Sat; 12 -11 Sun

Caledonian Deuchars IPA; Guest Beer (Occasional)[H] ☺

Originally a coaching inn dating from 1701 and popular with locals and visitors. The main bar boasts wooden beams and a real fire. There is also a large comfortable lounge. The gable end is a dining area which was originally a smithy. Naturally the décor consists of a hunting theme and old photographs of the area. There are also tankards, steins and saws.

AC OD (pavement tables & patio) ML (12-2.30) ME (6-8.30; 5-7.30 Sun) BS CW DW (bar only)

Broughton

Laurel Bank

By Biggar, ML12 6HF

(01899) 830462

Bus: McEwans 91, 199

11(12 Sun) - 11

Guest Beer (Jun-Oct)

Recently extended to include a bistro and bar. Good meals, prepared on the premises from local products.

DA OD MD BS CW

Carlops

Allan Ramsay Hotel

Main Street, EH26 9NF

(01968) 660258

12 - 11(1am Fri & Sat); 12.30 - Midnight Sun

Caledonian Deuchars IPA; Guest Beer[H] ☺

Hotel, in a small village beside the Pentland Hills, dating from 1792. Several rooms have been knocked

through into a single area, retaining many original features including a fine stone fireplace. Tartan upholstery gives a Scottish feel. One end is a restaurant, the central part is a bar area and a pool table occupies the far end. The bar is inlaid with pre-decimal pennies.

AC OD ML (12-3) ME (6-9) MD (12-9 Sat & Sun) BS CW DW

Chirnside

Chirnside Inn

Allanton Road, TD11 3XH (S edge of village)

(01890) 818034

Bus: First 60, 260; Waits 34

12-2.30 Wed & Thu, 5(12 Fri & Sat; 12.30 Sun)- Midnight

Caledonian Deuchars IPA; Hadrian & Border Farne Island; Guest Beer[H] ☺

This comfortable village local, formerly the Waterloo, features wood panelling and beamed ceiling. Prints of racing driver Jim Clark, whose family farmed nearby, adorn the walls. Said to be haunted.

AC OD (patio) ML (12-2.30; not Mon & Tue) ME (6-8.30) BS CW (until 9pm) DW (bar only)

Coldingham

Anchor Inn

School Road, TD14 5NS

(01890) 771243

Bus: Perrymans 235, 253

12 - Midnight(can be earlier in winter)

Beer Range (2 summer) Varies[H] ☺

Multi-roomed village local welcoming visitors and regulars alike. The bar is wood panelled while local photographs adorn the walls in the cosy well appointed lounge / dining room. There is a mirror recovered from the wreck of the Glenmire, which sank off St. Abbs head in 1910. The menu is extensive and has a good vegetarian selection. Take-aways are available.

OD (garden at rear, seats at front) ML ME BS CW (in lounge & dining room)

Coldstream

Besom

75 - 77 High Street, TD12 4AE

(01890) 882391

11(12.30 Sun) - Midnight(1am Fri & Sat)

Caledonian Deuchars IPA, XPA[H] ☺

Comfortable pub in historic Borders town, the first in Scotland! The walls are decorated with a diverse range of memorabilia, some related to the Coldstream Guards. The bar has a real fire, bookshelves, trophy cabinet and sofa-like seating which gives the feel of a living room as much as a pub. The rear lounge has fawn banquette seating.

OD (pavement tables and courtyard) ML (12-2) ME (6.30-8.30(9 Summer)) BS CW (not bar) DW (bar only)

Denholm

Auld Cross Keys Inn

Main Street, TD9 8NU

(01450) 870305

11(12.30 Sun) - 11(1am Fri & Sat)

Guest Beer[H] ☺

18th century inn by the village green. The cosy bar has a low ceiling, varnished pine plank walls and a lino tiled floor. At one end is the real fire, while the other has a pool table. To the rear is a more upmarket lounge and dining area, which can open out into a large function room. Quizzes, folk music sessions and concerts are regular events. Good home-cooked food is served and on Sun there is also a carvery.

AC OD (pavement tables) ML (12-2.30) ME (5.30-8) MD (1-7 Sun) BS CW DW (bar only)

Fox & Hounds Inn

Main Street, TD9 8NU

(01450) 870247

11-3, 5-Midnight(1am Fri); 11 - 1am Sat; 12.30 - Midnight Sun

Wylam Gold Tankard; Guest Beer[H] ☺

A village local, built 1728, overlooking the village green. The main bar is light and retains the original beams with a real fire giving it a cosy feel in winter.

Pictures and memorabilia decorate the walls. The rear lounge has a coffee house feel. An upstairs dining room is used in the evening.

AC OD (courtyard & garden) ML (12-2.30) ME (6-8) BS CW (until 8pm) DW

Duns

Black Bull Hotel

15 Black Bull Street, TD11 3AR

(01361) 883379

Bus: First 60

11(12.30 Sun) - Midnight(1am Fri & Sat)

Caledonian Deuchars IPA; Guest Beer (2 summer)[H] ☺

200 year old hotel with separate bar, lounge, restaurant and function room. The cosy front bar, popular with locals, has dark wood panelling and framed sketches, produced by a local artist, above the upright piano. The lounge area, with bench seating, is more suited to families. The refurbished letting rooms are all named after local historical figures.

AC OD (garden & patio) ML (12-2; 12.30-3 Sun) ME (6-9; 6-8 Sun) BS CW DW (bar only)

Whip & Saddle

Market Square, TD11 3BZ

(01361) 884455

Bus: First 60; Waites 260

12 - 11; 11 - 1am Fri & Sat; 12.30 - 11.30 Sun

Guest Beer[H]

Town centre bar, with plain but bright décor and wooden floor. The ornate gantry is a feature. The new licensee hopes to promote real ale and expand the food side.

ML (12-5) BS CW DW

Eddleston

Horseshoe Inn & Lodge

(01721) 730225

Bus: First 62

11(12 Sun) - 11; Closed Mon.

Draught Bass[H]

A sophisticated restauarant and bar serving award winning cuisine. The bar is used as a bistro, and with no sitting or standing at the bar, the best way to enjoy the Bass is with a meal. Better for drinkers to avoid peak meal times.

AC DA OD (courtyard) ML (12-2.30) ME (7-9; 6.30-9.30 Fri & Sat) CW

Ettrickbridge

Cross Keys Inn

Ettrickbridge, TD7 5JN

(01750) 52224

12(12.30 Sun)-2.30, 6.30-10.30(11 Thu-Sat); Closed Mon & Tue winter

Beer Range (2) Varies[H] ☺

17th century inn located in the historic Ettrick valley. The cosy main bar and adjacent dining room are decorated with old photographs, water jugs and the odd stuffed animal. There is a strong emphasis on quality food so tables are set for diners. The bar stools remain popular and there is a smaller room dedicated to drinkers with a TV. The real ales are often from smaller Scottish breweries such as Broughton and Inveralmond.

AC DA OD (benches at front & garden) ML (12(12.30 Sun)-1.45) ME (6.30-8.30(9 Fri & Sat)) BS CW

Eyemouth

Ship Hotel

Harbour Road, TD14 5HT

(01890) 750224

Bus: Perryman 235, 253

11(12 Sun) - Midnight(1am Fri & Sat)

Caledonian Deuchars IPA, 80[H]

Hotel with a busy functional bar and a lounge/restaurant which is brighter and much quieter. The bar offers views of activities in the harbour – if you are lucky you might see seals or a Chinese junk! Close to the World of Boats sailing craft museum.

AC OD (seats by front door) ML ME BS CW (until 8pm, in lounge

Flemington

First & Last

A1 road

(01890) 781306

Bus: Perryman's 235, 253

11-2, 4-Midnight; 11 - 1am Fri & Sat; 12.30 - 11 Sun

Inveralmond Ossian's Ale[H]

This pub, with bar, dining room and pool room, has recently started keeping real ale with considerable success. Frequented by locals and travellers on the adjacent A1. Decorated with old photographs and nautical artefacts.

DA OD (paved area with benches) ML (not Tue) ME (not Tue) MD (Fri-Sun) BS CW (until 8pm)

Galashiels

Hunter's Hall

56 High St., TD1 1SE (N end of centre)

(01896) 759795

Bus: First 8/8A, 9/9A, 60, 61,62, 68, 71, 73, 95/X95

11(12.30 Sun) - Midnight(1am Thu-Sat)

Greene King Abbot Ale; 2 Guest Beers[H] ☺

Originally built as a church, now converted by J D Wetherspoon into a single roomed pub with three main drinking areas. The front area has paintings by local artists on the walls and is a family area. The main bar area has bare stone walls, a trellis ceiling and historic photos of Galashiels. The third area has more historic photos of the town.

DA OD (small yard) MD (9-11) BS CW (until 8pm, if eating)

Ladhope Inn

33 High Buckholmside, TD1 2HR (A7, 1/2m N of centre)

(01896) 752446

Bus: First 95/X95

11-3, 5-11; 11 - 11 Wed; 11 - Midnight Thu-Sat; 12.30 - Midnight Sun

Caledonian Deuchars IPA; Guest Beer[H] ☺

Comfortable, friendly local with a vibrant Border's atmosphere. Originating circa 1792, it has been altered considerably inside and comprises of a single room, decorated with whisky jugs and a large inked map of the Galashiels area. A wee alcove has a golfing theme. Three flat screen TVs ensure the pub is busy during sporting events. The guest beer is often from Hadrian & Border but changes regularly.

OD CW DW

Salmon Inn

54 Bank Street, TD1 1EP (Opp. gardens & fountain)

(01896) 752577

Bus: First 8/8A, 9/9A, 60, 61,62, 68, 71, 73, 95/X95

11(12.30 Sun) - 11(Midnight Thu & Sun, 1am Fri & Sat)

Caledonian Deuchars IPA; 2 Guest Beers[H] ☺

Comfortable, friendly pub that can be very lively when sports events are on the flat screen TVs. The single room, decorated with historic photographs of the Galashiels area, is split into 2 areas. The guest beers, often from smaller breweries, change regularly. Popular for its good home cooked meals.

OD (garden) ML (12-2; not Sun) ME (5-8; not Sun) BS CW (lunchtime only) DW

Hawick

Callaghan's Irish Bar

20-22 High St., TD9 9EH

(01450) 379679

Bus: First 72, 73, 95/X95: Munro 20

12(12.30 Sun) - Midnight(1am Fri & Sat)

Beer Range (2) Varies[H] ☺

Popular, plain, High Street pub with bare wooden floor, wood panelling around the walls and rustic furniture. The decoration has a sporting theme with rugby jerseys on display. Several TV screens typically show racing, rugby or football on Sat. afternoon. Live music at weekends and a quiz on Thursday. Soup available at weekends.

DA OD (pavement tables) CW (until 8pm) DW

Conservative Club

Bourtree Place

(01450) 372089

Bus: First 72, 73, 95/X95: Munro 20

11(12.30 Sun) - Midnight (1am Fri & Sat)

Beer Range (2) Varies[H] ☺

Plush lounge bar and adjoining large snooker hall. There is a function room upstairs. WARNING: Entry restricted to members and guests. Check details before visit.

OD ML (Sat) DW (not Sat & Sun)

Innerleithen

St. Ronan's Hotel

High Street, EH44 6HF

(01896) 831487

Bus: First 62

11(12 Sun) - Midnight(12.45am Fri & Sat)

Guest Beer[H] ☺

This village hotel takes its name from the local Saint who is also associated with a well. The functional public bar is long and thin and has a brick and wooden fireplace. There are two alcoves, one with seating, the other with a dartboard and a wide angled photograph of the village. A room with a pool table leads off from this. Pick up service available for Southern Upland Way walkers.

AC OD MD (summer only) BS CW DW

Traquair Arms Hotel

Traquair Road, EH44 6PD

(01896) 830229

Bus: First 62

11 - 11(Midnight Fri & Sat); 12 - 11.30 Sun

Caledonian Deuchars IPA; Taylor Landlord; Traquair Bear Ale[H] ☺

Elegant 18th-century hotel in the scenic Tweed Valley. The comfortable lounge bar features a welcoming real fire in winter and a relaxing tropical fish tank. An Italian bistro area and separate restaurant provide plenty of room for diners. One of the few outlets for draft ales from Traquair House.

AC OD ML ME MD (Sat & Sun) BS CW

Jedburgh

Exchange Inn (Cannon)

8 Exchange Street, TD8 6BH

(01835) 863243

Bus: First 68, 71; Munro 20

11 - Midnight(1am Fri); 12.30 - 11 Sun

Theakstons Best Bitter; Guest Beer (summer)[H]

Compact town centre pub with a traditional atmosphere. WARNING: Check details before visit.

DW

Pheasant

61/63 High Street, TD8 6DQ

(01835) 862708

Bus: First/Munro 68, 51, 20, 81, 131

12-2.30, 5.30-11(Midnight Fri); 12 - 1am Sat; 12.30 - 11 Sun

Guest Beer[H]

Formerly the Liberal club, but now a spacious bar with contemporary interior. Chunky leather chairs and matching stools, plus a wood panelled floor all give a bright trendy appearance.

DA   ML (12-2.15)   ME (6-8.30)   BS   CW

Spreadeagle Hotel

20 High Street, TD8 6AG

(01835) 862870

Bus: First/Munro 68, 51, 20, 81, 131

12 - 11(Midnight Fri & Sat)

Guest Beer[H] ☺

Basic wood panelled public bar in a old Georgian facaded hotel. The beer is usually from Hadrian & Border brewery. Food times may vary out of season. Accomodation recently refurbished.

AC   OD (courtyard)   ML (12-2.30)   ME (6-9)   DW

Kelso

Cobbles Inn

7 Bowmont Street, TD5 7JH (off NE side of town square)

(01573) 223548

Bus: First / Munro 20, 55, 67

11-3, 5-10(1am Fri); All day summer; 11 - Midnight Sat; 11 - 10 Sun

Beer Range (2) Varies ☺

Completely refurbished in 2008, this gastro pub boasts a lounge bar with a huge open fire which will catch the eye on cold days. There is also a dining area, though one can eat anywhere. The bar menu features hearty favourites, whilst the dinner menu and daily specials board offer more adventurous dishes. A third pump is planned to expand the choice of interesting ales from both sides of the border. Private functions are catered for upstairs.

DA   OD   ML (12-2.30)   ME (6-9.30)   MD (Sat & Sun)   BS   CW

Queens Head Hotel

Bridge Street, TD5 7JD

(01573) 228899

Bus: First / Munro 20, 55, 67

11(12 Sun) - 11(11.45 Fri, 12.45am Sat)

Caledonian Deuchars IPA; Greene King Old Speckeled Hen[H] ☺

The split level bar and lounge/eating area of this historic inn have been transformed by a bright, contemporary make-over. The light wood panelled floors and part brick walls, gives it a brasserie feel.

AC   DA   MD (11-9.30)   BS

Waggon Inn

10 Coalmarket, TD5 7AH

(01573) 224568

Bus: First / Munro 20, 55, 67

11-3, 5-11; 11 - 1am Sat; 12 - Midnight Sun

Guest Beer[H] ☺

Popular with families and focusing on food, this community pub, with its two split level areas, also has live music on Friday nights. The guest beeer changes regularly.

DA   ML (12-2.30)   ME (5-9)   MD (12-9.30 Sat)   BS   CW (playroom)

White Swan

Abbey Row, TD5 7AT

(01573) 224348

Bus: First / Munro 20, 55, 67

11(12.30 Sun) - Midnight(1am Thu-Sat)

Caledonian Deuchars IPA; Tetley Bitter; Guest Beer[H]

A popular town local with bare wooden floor boards, exposed stone and a real fire. Pool is played in the back area.

BS   DW

Kirk Yetholm

Border Hotel

The Green, TD5 8PQ

(01573) 420237

11(12 Sun) - Midnight(1am Fri & Sat); Can close earlier in winter

Beer Range (2 summer) Varies [H] ☺

This 260 year old coaching inn is very popular with walkers, being situated at the beginning or end of the Pennine Way and on the ancient St Cuthbert's Way. The wood beamed bar has a roaring coal fire in winter and the walls are adorned with photographs of local worthies and friezes showing country pursuits. In addition, there are some smaller rooms and a conservatory dining area. The hotel has now recovered from a serious fire in 2006.

AC OD (garden & seats at front) ML (12-2) ME (6-9) BS CW DW (bar only)

Lauder

Black Bull Hotel

Market Place, TD2 6SR

(01578) 722208

11(12.30 Sun) - 11(Midnight Fri & Sat)

Beer Range (2) varies[H] ☺

Well-appointed old coaching inn. The small wood-panelled bar is adorned with artefacts and retains much of the character of yester-year. Leading off are various dining areas.

AC DA OD (picnic benches) ML (12.30-2.30) ME (5-9) BS CW DW

Eagle Hotel

1 Market Place, TD2 6SR

(01578) 722426

Bus: First / Munro 20, 51, 52, 61

11(12.30 Sun) - 11(Midnight Thu; 1am Fri & Sat)

Caledonian Deuchars IPA; Guest Beer[H]

A two roomed pub in centre of village. The stone wall surrounding the fire place and the ornate bar are features of the lounge. The more functional bar has an interesting mirror-backed gantry and a real fire.

OD (courtyard) ML (12-2 Fri & Sat) ME (6-9 Fri & Sat) MD (12-6 Sun) BS CW (lounge) DW (bar)

Golden Bannock

4 West High Street, TD2 6TE

(01578) 722324

Bus: First / Munro 20, 51, 52, 61

5(12.30 Sun) - 11; 3 - 1am Fri; 11 - 1am Sat

Tetley Bitter[H]

Cosy, small, locals pub in centre of village with a functional bar and pool room. Pictures of the common ridings adorn the walls.

OD (pavement tables) DW

Leitholm

Plough Hotel

Main Street, TD12 4JN

(01890) 840252

12(4.30 Mon & Tue) - Midnight(1am Fri & Sat)

Beer Range (2 summer) varies[H] ☺

19th century terraced pub on main street of quiet Borders village. The simple, plain interior is comfortably furnished and decorated with prints of local scenes. The real fire, in winter at least, and the resident Golden Retriever give a domestic and appealing atmosphere. Changes planned for summer 2008 will reduce the pub to a single bar area.

OD BS CW (until 9pm) DW (very)

Melrose

Burt's Hotel

Market Square, TD6 9PL

(01896) 822285

Bus: Most Melrose Buses

11(12 Sun)-2, 5(6 Sun)-11

Caledonian Deuchars IPA, 80; Guest Beer[H]

Elegant, family run hotel in the main square. The restaurant serves excellent food but is expensive. Cheaper options are available in the plush lounge bar.

AC OD (garden) ML ME BS CW DW

George & Abbotsford Hotel

High St., TD6 9PD

(01896) 822308

Bus: Most Melrose buses

11(12 Sun) - 11(Midnight Fri & Sat)

Beer Range (2) Varies[H]

Comfortable bar overlooking the main street and serving a varying range of real ales, often from smaller breweries. Adjacent to the bar is a shop selling a range of bottled beers.

AC OD (garden) MD (12-8.30) BS CW DW

King's Arms Hotel

High Street, TD6 9PB

(01896) 822143

Bus: Most Melrose buses

11(12 Sun) - 11(Midnight Fri & Sat)

Caledonian Deuchars IPA; Greene King Old Speckled Hen; Guest Beer[H] ☺

Old coaching inn dating from 1793. The bar has a wooden floor and church pew seating, and is decorated with rugby memorabilia and old local photographs. There is a large-screen TV for sports events. The quieter lounge is comfortably furnished and has a lovely old carved door set into the ceiling. There are also dining rooms upstairs. National Cycle Route 1 passes the door.

AC   ML (12-2)   ME (6.30-9; 5.30-8.30 Sun)   BS   CW (until 8pm, lounge)   DW

Townhouse Hotel

Market Square, TD6 9PQ

(01896) 822645

Bus: Most Melrose buses

11(12 Sun)-2.30, 5(6 Sun)-11

Caledonian Deuchars IPA[H]

The bar is a contemporary brassiere, serving innovative lunches and dinners. A restaurant offers a more formal atmosphere. WARNING: Diners have priority at busy times.

AC   OD (patio)   ML (12-2)   ME (6-9)   BS   CW

Mountbenger

Gordon Arms Hotel

Mountbenger, TD7 5LE

(01750) 82222

11 - 11(1am Fri & Sat; 10 Sun); Closed Mon & Tue in winter

Guest Beer (May-Sep)[H]

This welcoming hotel is situated on the Southern upland way. There is a small cosy bar area and a larger lounge and dining room. A converted hayloft offers low cost accommodation. WARNING: Due to reopen Summer 08 following fire damage. Check details before visit.

AC   OD   MD (until 9)   BS   CW   DW

Newcastleton

Liddesdale Hotel

Douglas Square, TD9 0QD

(01387) 375255

11(12 Sun) - 11(1am Fri & Sat)

Beer Range (1 winter, 2 summer) Varies[H] ☺

Hotel, with a bright split level bar, in the main square of a remote 18th century planned weaver's village. The upper level, with a real fire, serves as a dining area while the lower area near the bar has art-deco style wooden panelling. Prints of London adorn the walls and the encyclopaedia Britannica is available for reference.

AC   DA   OD (garden & tables at front and back)   ML (12-2)   ME (6-9)   BS   CW (until 8pm, in lounge)   DW

Paxton

Cross Inn

Paxton, TD15 1TE

(01289) 386267

11(12.30 Sun)-3, 6.30-Midnight; Closed Mon

Stewart Pentland IPA; Guest Beer[H] ☺

Friendly village pub, circa 1870s, named after the restored old cross outside. The wooden panelled bar has a bright but intimate feel, a south facing bay window providing plenty of light. The guest beer is often from Wylam. Popular for food, there is an appealing, extensive menu featuring home cooked dishes using local sourced ingredients. A small dining room provides a more formal eating area.

DA (access at rear)   OD (patio)   ML (12-2)   ME (6.30(5.30 Fri)-9)   BS   CW   DW

Bridge Inn – CAMRA 2008 Borders Pub of the Year runner up and past winner

Peebles

Bridge Inn

Portbrae, EH45 8AW

(01721) 720589

Bus: First 62

11(12.30 Sun) - Midnight

Caledonian Deuchars IPA; Stewart Pentland IPA; Taylor Landlord; Tweedside Ale (Stewart No 3); Guest Beer[H] ☺

Cheerful, welcoming, single roomed, town-centre local, also known as the `Trust`. The mosaic entrance floor shows it was once the Tweedside Inn. The bright, comfortable bar is decorated with jugs, bottles, memorabilia of outdoor pursuits and photos of old Peebles. An outdoor heated patio area overlooks the river. The gents is superb, with well maintained original Twyford Adamant urinals. Runner up of CAMRA Borders Pub of the Year 2008 competition.

OD (patio) DW

County Inn

High St., EH45 8AN

(01721) 720595

Bus: First 62

11(12.30 Sun) - Midnight(1am Thu-Sat)

Beer Range (3) Varies[H]

Large popular pub divided into several rooms. The recent refurbishment blends well with the original features, such as a low sunken room with a barrel-vaulted ceiling.

DA   MD (12-7.45) BS CW   DW

Cross Keys Hotel

Northgate, EH45 8RS

(01721) 724222

Bus: First 62

12(12.30 Sun) - Midnight(1am Sat)

Stewart Pentland IPA; Guest Beer[H] ☺

Old coaching Inn, just off the High Street, with a large L shaped lounge bar. The ceiling is low but the light coloured decor gives a spacious feel. The

imposing bar and gantry were reclaimed from a demolished Edinburgh pub. Although generally relaxed it can be lively during weekend evenings.

DA OD DW

Crown Hotel

High Street, EH45

(01721) 720239

Bus: First 62

11 - Midnight

Beer Range Varies[H] ☺

A narrow basic bar opens out to a seating area with a leather settee and banquettes. There are wooden floors and half panelled walls throughout. To the rear is a lovely restaurant area with a conservatory attached. The bar is very popular with the locals, who make visitors welcome. WARNING: Real ale not always available in winter.

AC OD MD BS CW DW

Neidpath Inn

27- 29 Old Town, EH45 8JF

(01721) 724306

Bus: First 62

11(12.30 Sun) - Midnight(1am Fri & Sat)

Caledonian Deuchars IPA, 80; Guest Beer (occasional)[H]

The bar of this unassuming pub has seating areas, a pool table, darts board and a very attractive mahogany mirrored gantry. The comfortable lounge leads into an eating area with an outdoor decked area.

AC DA OD ML (12-2) ME (5-9) MD (12-9 Sat; 12.30-8.30 Sun) BS CW (until 7pm, not in bar) DW (bar only)

Tontine Hotel

High Street, EH45 8AJ

(01721) 720892

Bus: First 62

11(12 Sun) - 11

Guest Beer[H]

Plush, tweedy, Borders town hotel. The cosy wood panelled bar, with marble topped counter, is decorated with local prints of historic interest. The beer is usually from Broughton Brewery.

AC DA ML (12-2) ME (6-9) BS CW (lounge)

Reston

Red Lion

Main St., TD14 5JP

(01890) 761266

Bus: Perrymans 253

12(12.30 Sun)-2.30, 5.30-11; 12 - Midnight Fri & Sat; Closed Mon

Beer Range Varies[H]

Comfortable pub well signposted from the nearby A1. An area is set aside for eating and the menu is good and varied. The lounge bar features wooden bench seating, a real fire and an intriguing collection of vintage cameras. During Jan, food is only served Sat & Sun lunch.

AC DA OD (garden) ML ME BS CW

Selkirk

Heatherlie House Hotel

Heatherlie Park, TD7 5AL

(01750) 721200

Bus: First 72, 95

12(12.30 Sun) - 11(Midnight Fri-Sun)

Guest Beer[H] ☺

A family run hotel in tranquil surroundings. Once a Victorian villa, it retains a stately air of grandeur with a magnificent hand carved fireplace depicting barn owls in the entrance and beautiful cornices. The bar, which is also a dining area, is comfortable and airy. It has views through the large bay windows to the gardens. The real ale is often from Inveralmond or Stewart Brewing.

AC OD ML (12-2) ME (6-9) BS CW

Town Arms

1 Market Place, TD7 4BT

(01750) 20185

Bus: First 72, 73, 95

11(12.30 Sun) - Midnight(1am Fri & Sat)

Guest Beer[H]

A small locals' pub, situated just off the market square. The interior is very traditional with wood panelled walls adorned with numerous brewery mirrors and is dominated by a large island bar.

DW

St Boswells

Buccleuch Arms

St. Boswells, TD6 0EW (On A68)

(01835) 822243

Bus: Munro C3, 29, 30, 67, 68

11(12 Sun) - 11

Guest Beer[H]

Well appointed hotel by the village green and cricket ground. The lounge bar, with its wood panelling and sporting / hunting prints, focuses on food. The real ale hand pump is not easily seen.

AC (19 en-suite rooms) DA   OD (garden)   ML (12-2) ME (6-9) BS CW DW

St. Mary's Loch

Tibbie Shiels Inn

St Mary's Loch, TD7 5LH (Off A708 at southern end of loch)

(01750) 42231

11(12.30 Sun) - 11(Midnight Fri & Sat); Closed Mon-Wed between Nov & Easter

Belhaven 80/-; Broughton Greenmantle IPA[H]

A cosy, characterful, isolated, historic inn in the remote Yarrow Valley on the Southern Upland Way. WARNING: Changing hands in June 08 so details may change.

AC DA   OD   MD (12.30-7.45) BS CW (until 8.30)

Swinton

Wheatsheaf Hotel

Main Street, TD11 3JJ

(01890) 860257

11(12.30 Sun) - 11

Caledonian Deuchars IPA[H]   ☺

This well appointed hotel focuses on good food. There are three large comfortable dining and lounge areas, one being a conservatory. WARNING: Drinkers may not be welcome at peak meal times.

AC DA   ML (12-2) ME (6-9) CW

Town Yetholm

Plough Hotel

High Street, TD5 8RF

(01573) 420215

Bus: First 81

11 - Midnight(1am Fri & Sat)

2 Guest Beers[H]

Friendly village inn set in rural surroundings and near the end of the Pennine Way walk. The bar has mock Tudor décor and a huge wood burning stove. Also has small dining and games rooms. The food is jolly good and portions plentiful.

AC DA   OD (garden at back, tables at front) ML (12-2.30) ME (6-8.30) BS CW (until 8pm) DW

Tweedsmuir

Crook Inn

TWEEDSMUIR, ML12 6QN

(01899) 880272

Dating back to 1604, the current building is mainly 1930s art deco, and such a good example it is listed in CAMRA's national pub inventory. WARNING: Currently closed and focus of a local campaign to prevent it being turned into flats.

West Linton

Gordon Arms Hotel

Dolphinton Road, EH46 7DR

(01968) 660208

Bus: MacEwans 100 (Ed - Dumfries)

11(12 Sun) - 11(Midnight Tue; 1am Fri & Sat)

Stewart Pentland IPA; Guest Beer[H]   ☺

Situated in a village close to the Pentland Hills. The public bar is L shaped with stone walls and interesting cornice. A homely feel is created by a real fire and a collection of sofas and chairs. A jukebox and TV provide entertainment. The attractive, comfortable restaurant has wooden floors and neatly arranged dining tables.

AC OD   ML (12-3) ME (6-9) MD (12-9 Sat & Sun) BS CW DW

Aberlady

Kilspindie House Hotel

Main Street, EH32 0RE

(01875) 870682

Bus: First 124, X5

12(12.30 Sun) - Midnight

Caledonian Deuchars IPA (summer only)[H]

Hotel with a good reputation for food. The bar has fine mirrors from Binnies brewery of Haddington and a selection of distilleries. Several restaurant cum dining areas lead off.

AC DA OD (courtyard) ML (12-3) ME (5-10) MD (12-10 Sun) BS CW (until 8pm, not bar) DW

Auchendinny

Victoria

39 The Brae, EH26 0QU

(01968) 673088

Bus: Lothian 15; First 141

12(11 Sat; 12.30 Sun) - 11(1am Fri & Sat)

Beer Range Varies[H] (Often Ossian's) ☺

Community oriented pub with public bar and small restaurant. The bar is Tudor style with wooden beams and floor. A wooden gantry sits behind the upholstered counter front. A large wooden Red Indian guards the doors to the garden. There is a dart board and pool table and pictures on the wall. The restaurant is half wood panelled and has a real fire.

OD (garden & patio) MD (12.30-6) BS CW (until 8pm) DW

Balerno

Grey Horse

20 Main Street, EH14 7EH

(0131) 449 2888

Bus: Lothian 44/44A, N44; Prentice 424

10(12.30 Sun) - 1am

Caledonian Deuchars IPA; Guest Beer[H] ☺

200 year old traditional stone built village centre pub. The public bar retains some original features with wood panelling and a fine Bernard's mirror. A carpet gives a warm ambiance. The lounge is pleasantly decorated and has green banquette seating. The café next door is part of the pub so you can have a drink with your meal.

ML ME BS CW (until 8pm, in lounge) DW

Malleny Arms

15 Main St., EH14 7EQ

(0131) 449 7795

Bus: Lothian 44/44A, N44; Prentice 424

11 - Midnight; 12.30 - 11 Sun

Caledonian Deuchars IPA[H] ☺

This one time hotel, also known as "Honky Tonk" is situated in Balerno's pedestrian area. A vibrant community pub with weekly "honky" pool competitions. Large screen TVs also make it popular on sporting occasions. Light wood floors and décor along with an area of comfy settees give a bright but homely feel.

OD DW

Bathgate

James Young

6-40 Hopetoun Street, EH48 4EU

Bus: First 9, 10, 27

9am - 11(1am Fri & Sat)

Caledonian Deuchars IPA; 3 Guest Beers[H]

Lloyds No.1 pub attracting a wide range of customers. Raised floor levels at rear and comfortable armchairs for those who wish to relax over their food and drink.

DA OD (at rear) MD BS CW

Belhaven

Masons Arms

8 High Street, EH42 1NP (A1087, 1m W of Dunbar.)

(01368) 863700

Bus: First 44d, X6; Perrymans 253

12-3, 5-11; 12 - Midnight Fri & Sat; 12.30 - 11 Sun

Belhaven 80/-; Guest Beer[H] ☺

Friendly pub close to Belhaven Brewery with fine views to the Lammermuir Hills. The bright, comfortable public bar is surrounded with banquette seating and the floor is laid with a quality wood laminate. The walls are hung with pictures of old sailing ships. There is also a pleasant dining room where food from a good menu is served. The guest beer is from the Belhaven or Greene King guest lists.

OD   ML   ME (not Sun) BS

Bonnyrigg

Retreat Castle Hotel

1 Cockpen Road, EH19 3HS

(0131) 660 3200

Bus: Lothian 31(B'rigg); N31

12 - 1am(Midnight Sun)

Caledonian Deuchars IPA; Guest Beer (summer)[H]

Impressive castle like building with bar, dining room and conservatory restaurant. The bar is decorated with a vast array of pictures and artefacts. There is also a chapel if you fancy getting married.

AC DA   OD (garden & play area) MD (12-closing) BS CW (until 9pm)

Cockenzie

Thorntree Inn

100 High Street (by Port Seton on map)

(01875) 812782

Bus: Lothian 26 (S' Sands), N26

11(12.30 Sun) - 11(11.30 Thu; 12.30am Fri & Sat)

Caledonian Deuchars IPA[H]

Friendly, well run pub with views over the Firth of Forth.

DA BS CW DW

Currie

Riccarton Arms Inn

198 Lanark Road West, EH14 5NX

(0131) 449 2230

Bus: Lothian 44/44A, 45, N44

11 - 11(Midnight Fri & Sat)

Caledonian Deuchars IPA; Guest Beer[H]

Long thin lounge bar with semi enclosed seating area at one end and "half timbered" effect walls & ceilings. A community pub with weekly quiz night, live entertainment, TVs for sport, dart board and Wii 10-Pin bowling every Mon.

AC (5 rooms) OD (bench seats at rear) MD (12(12.30 Sun)-8) BS CW DW

Dalkeith

Blacksmith's Forge

Newmills Road, EH22 1DU

(0131) 561 5100

Bus: Lothian 3/3A, N3; First 86, 79, 90, 110

9am - Midnight(1am Fri & Sat)

Caledonian Deuchars IPA; Greene King Abbot; 2 Guest Beers[H]

J D Wetherspoon establishment with a mixture of differently styled seating areas. Mirrors and artwork adorn the walls. 2 small TVs and a gaming machine, but otherwise reasonably quiet.

DA   OD (paved area at front) MD BS CW

Buccleuch

90 High Street

(0131) 660 4840

Bus: Lothian 3/3A, N3; First 86, 79, 90, 110

11 - 11(1am Fri & Sat)

Caledonian Deuchars IPA, 80[H]

Large, modern style, open plan pub. Busy, especially when football is on the six+ TV screens. A small corner has a more traditional feel, with a fireplace and large mirror.

DA MD BS CW

Volunterer Arms – CAMRA 2008 Lothians Pub of the Year runner up

Dunbar

New Bayswell Hotel

Bayswell Park, EH42 1AE (on clifftop, W of centre)

(01368) 862225

Bus: First 44D, 106; Perrymans 253

12-3, 6-11

Caledonian Deuchars IPA[P]

Comfortable hotel with magnificent cliffside location. WARNING: Cask ale is only available in the upstairs lounge that is not always open. Phone to check.

AC OD (picnic benches) ML (12-2) ME (6-8.30) BS CW

Rocks

Marine Road, EH42 1AR (on clifftop, W of centre)

(01368) 862287

Bus: First 44D, 106; Perrymans 253

11(12.30 Sun) - 11

Beer Range (2) Varies[H] ☺

Imposing "Scottish Riviera" red stone villa, now a hotel. Set back from the cliffs but with panoramic views across Dunbar bay. The well appointed bar has a high ceiling and dark wood décor. Several dining areas lead off. The friendly staff are happy to offer advice on the adventurous seafood orientated menu. Some items are expensive, but expect excellent quality. A wide variety of real ales are served on the 2 handpumps.

AC OD (patio at front & garden) ML (12-2) ME (5.30-9) BS CW

Volunteer Arms

17 Victoria Street, EH42 1HP (near swimming pool)

(01368) 862278

Bus: First 44D, 106   Rail: Dunbar

12 - 11(Midnight Thu; 1am Fri & Sat); 12.30 - Midnight Sun

Beer Range (2) Varies[H] ☺

Close to Dunbar harbour, this is a friendly traditional locals pub. The cosy panelled bar is decorated with lots of fishing and lifeboat orientated memorabilia.

The 2 real ales are usually from smaller breweries. Local real cider is occasionally available. Upstairs is a restaurant serving an excellent menu with an emphasis on seafood. CAMRA 2008 Lothian Pub of the Year runner up.

OD (patio at front) ML (12-3 winter) ME (6-9 winter) MD (until 9.30 summer) BS CW (until 8pm) DW (after 9pm)

East Linton

Crown

25-27 Bridge Street, EH40 3AG

(01620) 860335

Bus: First X6, X8; Perrymans 253

11(12 Winter) - 11(1am Thu-Sat; Midnight Sun)

Adnams Broadside; Caledonian Deuchars IPA; 2 Guest Beers[H] ☺

Small 18c stone built hotel in centre of historic conservation village. The functional, cosy bar has real log fire, lots of wood panelling and original Dudgeon brewery windows. To the rear is a large lounge / restaurant that serves good quality pub food from an imaginative menu. One of the guest beers is usually from Stewart Brewing.

AC OD ML ME (Winter, Thu-Sat only) MD (summer) BS CW DW

Drovers Inn

5 Bridge Streeet, EH40 3AG

(01620) 860298

Bus: First X6, X8; Perrymans 253

A village pub full of character with emphasis on food and was serving up to four serious ales. WARNING: Currently closed.

Linton Hotel

3 Bridge End, EH40 3AF

(01620) 860202

Bus: First X6, X8; Perrymans 253

12-2, 5-11; 12 - 11 Sun

Beer Range Varies[H]

Popular small hotel with excellent reputation for reasonably priced restaurant quality meals. There is a dining room and a quiet, comfortable bar which is also used as an overflow for diners.

AC DA ML ME BS CW

Edinburgh

56 North   J8

West Crosscauseway, EH8 9JP

(0131) 662 8860

Bus: Lothian 41, 42

9(12.30 Sun) - 1am

Caledonian Deuchars IPA, 80[P]

Modern, single roomed, food orientated bar with slate and wood facia. There is a TV and discreet background music. Popular with students.

OD MD (10-10) BS CW

99 Hanover St.   F2

99 Hanover Street

(0131) 225 8200

Bus: City Centre Rail: Waverley

12 - 1am

Caledonian Deuchars IPA[P]

Stylish bar with extravagent camp décor. Younger clientele and DJs. The food menus are pasted into old annuals.

DA MD (12-10) CW

Abbey Bar   U6

65 South Clerk Street, EH8 9PP

(0131) 668 4862

Bus: Lothian 3/3A, 5, 7, 8, 14, 29, 30, 31, 33, 37, 47, 49, N3, N8, N30, N31, N37

11(12.30 Sun) - Midnight

Caledonian Deuchars IPA; 2 Guest Beers[H]

Wooden floored alehouse, divided by an island bar, with decor typical of the chain. The pub is machine mad with 7 TV's along with fruit/quiz and pinball machines. Reasonably priced food.

DA OD (pavement tables) MD (12(12.30 Sun)-9(8 Sat & Sun)) BS CW (if eating)

Abbotsford Bar & Restaurant   G2

3 Rose Street, EH2 2PR

(0131) 225 5276

Bus: City Centre Rail: Waverley

11(12.30 Sun) - 11(Midnight Fri)

Beer Range (5) Varies[A] ☺

A traditional Scottish bar listed on CAMRA's national pub inventory. The magnificent island bar and gantry have been a fixture since 1902. The ornate plasterwork and corniced ceiling are highlighted by subdued lighting. The beers are often from micro-breweries. Evening meals are only served in the upstairs restaurant, but you may ask for beer from downstairs.

ML (12-3) ME (5.30-9.30 (restaurant only)) BS DW (after 3pm)

Advocate
I5

7 Hunters Square, EH1 1QW

(0131) 226 2749

Bus: Lothian 3/3A, 5, 7, 8, 14, 29, 30, 31, 33, 35, 37, 47, X47, X48, 49, N3, N8, N30, N31, N37 Rail: Waverley

10 - 1am

Caledonian Deuchars IPA, 80; Guest Beer[H]

Comfortable, city centre,food orientated, single roomed pub with small partitioned areas. Paintings, clocks and old radios are prominent. Open mike sessions on Thu. evening and a couple of gamming machines.

DA MD (10-10; not Sun) BS CW (until 8pm)

Albanach
I4

197 High Street, EH1 1PE

(0131) 220 5277

Bus: Lothian 3/3A, 5, 7, 8, 14, 29, 30, 31, 33, 35, 37, 47, X48, 49, N3, N8, N30, N31, N37 Rail: Waverley

10 - 1am

Belhaven 80/-; Caledonian Deuchars IPA; Greene King Abbot Ale[H] ☺

Modernised, chic bar with unusual beer founts.

OD MD (10-9)

Antiquary
S4

72 St. Stephen Street, EH3 5AQ

(0131) 225 2858

Bus: Lothian 24, 29, 36, 42

11.30 - 12.30am(1am Thu-Sat)

Caledonian Deuchars IPA; Guest Beer[H]

Wood-panelled basement bar with a number of interesting rooms, each with its own ambience, in particular a fine room at the rear. Tue. poker league,

Wed. quiz night and Thu. for folk music. Free Wi-Fi access.

OD (small) ML (12-3; not Fri) MD (12-6 Sat; 11-6 Sun) BS DW

Artisan
U4

35 London Road, EH7 5BQ

(0131) 661 1603

Bus: Lothian 1, 4, 5, 15/15A, 19, 26, 34, 35, 44/44A, 45, N26, N44

11 - 11.45; 12.30 - Midnight Sun

Caledonian Deuchars IPA[H]

A traditional bar, with ornate exterior, in a busy area near Hibs football ground. The interior has an island bar. Sunday night is quiz night.

DW

Athletic Arms (Diggers)
R6

1-3 Angle Park Terrace, EH11 2JX

(0131) 337 3822

Bus: Lothian 1, 34, 35 Rail: Haymarket

11(12.30 Sun) - Midnight

Caledonian Deuchars IPA, 80; Stewart Diggers 80/-[A]; 2 Guest Beers[H] ☺

Situated between two graveyards, the name 'Diggers' became synonymous with this Edinburgh legend, which opened in 1897. Banquette seating lines the walls and a compass drawing in the floor provides direction for the geographically challenged. Amongst the pictures and memorabilia, a brass wall plaque makes for interesting reading. A smaller back room houses a dartboard and further seating. Quieter now than in its heyday, but the pub still extends a warm welcome to local characters and visitors alike.

BS DW

Au Bar
A5

101 Shandwick Place, EH2 4SD

(0131) 228 2648

Bus: City Centre Rail: Haymarket

11(12 Sun) - Midnight(1am Fri & Sat)

Caledonian Deuchars IPA, 80; Guest Beer[H]

Large lounge bar with wooden decor and friendly atmosphere. Popular with office workers for food at lunchtime.

DA OD (at rear) MD (11-10) BS DW

Auld Hoose

U6

23 St. Leonards Street, EH8 9QN

(0131) 668 2934

Bus: Lothian 2

11.30(12.30 Sun) - 12.45am

Caledonian Deuchars IPA; Guest Beer[H] ☺

Traditional pub dating back to 1860's with large central U shaped bar and lots of pictures of old Edinburgh. Located in the student quarter, this is a friendly pub with a wide clientele. Try the alternative juke box, have a game of darts with the locals or enter the quiz on Tue evenings. Good pub food is served, including vegetarian and vegan options. The guest beer is usually from a Scottish micro. Free Wi-Fi access.

DA MD (until 9.30(8.30 Sun)) BS DW

Auld Toll

S6

37-39 Leven Street, EH3 9LN

(0131) 229 1010

Bus: Lothian 10, 11, 15/15A, 16, 17, 23, 27, 45, N11, N16, N27

11(12.30 Sun) - 11.45(12.45am Fri & Sat)

Caledonian Deuchars IPA[H]

U-shaped room, with traditional public bar area to the front and a cosier lounge tucked behind the bar gantry.

DA OD (garden at rear) CW (lounge during day) DW

Baillie

S4

2 St. Stephen Street, EH3 5AL

(0131) 225 4673

Bus: Lothian 24, 29, 36, 42

11(12.30 Sun) - Midnight(1am Fri & Sat)

Caledonian Deuchars IPA, 80, XPA; Courage Director's; Harviestoun Ptarmigan; Guest Beer[H]

New Town basement pub with large island bar and interesting Victorian print above the fireplace. Further sepia prints adorn the walls. Good food and a warm atmosphere, provided by the real fire.

OD (front basement) MD (until 9) BS CW (until 8pm, if eating) DW (bar area only)

Bank Hotel

J4

1-3 South Bridge, EH1 1LL

(0131) 556 9940

Bus: Lothian 3/3A, 5, 7, 8, 14, 29, 30, 31, 33, 35, 37, 47, X47, X48, 49, N3, N8, N30, N31, N37 Rail: Waverley

9am - 1am

Caledonian Deuchars IPA [H] ☺

Originally a bank, now refurbished as a hotel. The bar has additional seating on a mezzanine floor above the wood panelled bar and large screens for major sports events. Live music on Sundays.

AC OD (pavement tables) MD (9-9) BS CW (until 9pm)

Bannermans

J5

212 Cowgate, EH1 1NQ

(0131) 556 3254

Bus: Lothian 3/3A, 5, 7, 8, 14, 29, 30, 31, 33, 35, 37, 47, X47, X48, 49, N3, N8, N30, N31, N37 (to Tron) Rail: Waverley

12(12.30 Sun) - 1am

Caledonian Deuchars IPA, 80; Williams Fraoch[H] ☺

Located in the catacombs of the old town, Bannermans is well known for its live, often rock, music 6 nights a week. Tuesday evening is for student karaoke. A warren of vaulted rooms, bare stone walls, flagstone floors and ceilings draped with flags and posters give the pub a unique atmosphere. Free Wi-Fi access.

BS DW

Banter

B8

85-87 Fountainbridge, EH3 9PU

(0131) 228 8793

Bus: Lothian 1, 34, 35 Rail: Haymarket

12(12.30 Sun) - 1am

Caledonian Deuchars IPA; Guest Beer[H] ☺

The Auld Clachan was remodelled as the Banter in 2007. It now tries to create a traditional atmosphere with a modern edge to appeal to the wide clientele now working and living nearby. The inside is deceptively spacious with an "L" shaped bar and seating ranging from high stools to comfortable arm chairs. All live sports are shown and there is live music on Thu. and Sat. The home made meals include steak and guest ale pie.

DA MD (until 10) BS CW (until 8pm)

Barony Bar T4

81 - 85 Broughton Street, EH1 3RJ

(0131) 558 2874

Bus: Lothian 8, 17 (or 4, 10, 11, 12, 15/15A, 16, 26, 44/44A, 45 to York Place) Rail: Waverley

11(12.30 Sun) - Midnight(1am Fri & Sat)

Caledonian Deuchars IPA, 80; Black Sheep Bitter; Theakstons Old Peculier; 3 Guest Beers[H] ☺

Characterful city pub listed on the Scottish pub inventory due to its many fine internal features. Splendid tile work and stained wood are much in evidence while the bar and gantry are also noteworthy. Detailed cornices and a wooden floor add to the atmosphere of the L-shaped bar. Magnificent whisky mirrors adorn the walls.

DA OD (pavement tables) MD (until 10(7 Sun)) BS

Beehive Inn F6

18-20 Grassmarket, EH1 2JU

(0131) 225 7171

Bus: Lothian 2 (or 23, 27, 41, 42, 45, N27 to George IV Bridge) Rail: Waverley

11(12.30 Sun) - Midnight(1am Fri & Sat)

Caledonian Deuchars IPA; Guest Beer[H] ☺

On the site of a 16th century inn, the Beehive is a large, multi-roomed pub and restaurant. The upstairs restaurant features the condemned cell door from the old Tolbooth. Music, with DJ, on Fri. and Sat. evenings caters for Hen and Stag parties and ensures a lively, but rather noisy, atmosphere. The beer garden has great views up to the castle. Free Wi-Fi access.

DA OD (garden & pavement tables) MD (until 10) BS CW (until 8pm)

Bennets Bar S6

8 Leven Street, EH3 9LG

(0131) 229 5143

Bus: Lothian 10, 11, 15/15A, 16, 17, 23, 27, 45, N11, N16, N27

11 - 12.30am(1am Thu-Sat); 12 - 11.30 Sun

Caledonian Deuchars IPA, 80[H] ☺

Quite simply the zenith of late Victorian Edinburgh pub architecture, from the Jeffrey's Brewery etched door panels and window screens to the magnificent gantry. Whilst the Bernard's Brewery mirror at the end of the bar is the most spectacular, the Taylor McLeod mirrors are the most significant, being the last trace of the brewery that once stood on the site of the adjacent Kings Theatre.

ML (12-2; not Sun) ME (5-8.30; not Sun) BS CW (until 9pm, in green room if eating)

Bennet's Bar S8

1 Maxwell Street, EH10 5HT

(0131) 447 1903

Bus: Lothian 5, 11, 15/15A, 16, 17, 23, N11, N16

11 - Midnight; Closed Sun

Green King IPA; Inveralmond Ossian; 4 Guest Beers[A] ☺

Couthy back street boozer in the wealthy suburb of Morningside, yet it is only yards from one of the city's main trunk roads south. The pub has been owned by the eponymous family for generations and retains many features from the last major refurbishment some fifty years ago. The walls are adorned with photographs of old Edinburgh, including some of the long gone original Bennet's, next to Waverley station.

OD (pavement tables) BS

Bert's Bar S4

2/4 Raeburn Place, EH4 1HN

(0131) 343 3000

Bus: Lothian 24, 29, 36, 42

11(10 Sat, 12.30 Sun) - Midnight(1am Fri & Sat)

Caledonian Deuchars IPA; 4 Guest Beers[H] ☺

Refurbished sometime ago to resemble basic 60's boozer. A busy local, decorated with sporting bric-a-brac, 2 Murray's and 1 Ushers mirrors. Good choice of guest beers.

OD (pavement tables) MD (12-9) BS

Bert's Bar S5

29 - 31 William Street, EH3 7NG

(0131) 225 5748

Bus: Lothian 3/3A, 4, 12, 25, 26, 31, 33, 44/44A, X48, N25, N26, N31 Rail: Haymarket

11 - 11(1am Thu-Sat); 12.30 - Midnight Sun

Caledonian Deuchars IPA, 80; Harvieston Bitter & Twisted, Schiehallion; Taylor Landlord; 2 Guest Beers[H] ☺

Recreation of a traditional Scots' bar with quality wood and tile work. There is ample standing room, two sitting areas. Brewery mirrors feature and complement an excellent gantry. Good food served, why not try a pie.

MD (12-9) BS DW (on lead)

Black Bull   F6

12 Grassmarket, EH1 2JU

(0131) 225 6636

Bus: Lothian 2 (or 23, 27, 41, 42, 45, N27 to George IV Bridge) Rail: Waverley

11(10 Sun) - 1am

Caledonian Deuchars IPA; Courage Directors; Theakston Black Bull, Old Peculier[H]

Below the castle rock, this pub has a long L shaped bar with two small mezzanines. Bare boards surround the bar while the extensive seated areas are carpeted. Lots of T&J Bernard (an extinct Edinburgh brewery) memorabilia. 5 TV screens regularly show sport. It can be very lively on Fri & Sat evenings, with a mainly younger clientele and music provided by a DJ.

DA OD (pavement tables) MD (11-9) BS CW (until 8pm)

Black Rose   E3

49 Rose Street, EH2 2NH

(0131) 220 0414

Bus: City Centre Rail: Waverley

11(12.30 Sun) - 1am

Caledonian Deuchars IPA[H]

City centre bar featuring Tue open mic session and Wed quiz followed by Rock karaoke.

OD (pavement tables) ML ME BS

Blind Beggar   T3

97-99 Broughton Rd., EH7 4EG

(0131) 557 3130

Bus: Lothian 13, 36

12(1 Sun) - Midnight(1am Fri & Sat)

Caledonian Deuchars IPA[A]

Basic bar decorated with motorcycle parts and picture discs. The jukebox is turned up loud at weekends. The pub is not recommended for those with an aversion to heavy metal.

ML ME BS DW

Blind Poet   U6

32 West Nicolson Street, EH8 9DD

(0131) 667 4268

Bus: Lothian 2, 3/3A, 5, 7, 8, 14, 29, 30, 31, 33, 37, 47, X48, 49, N3, N8, N30, N31, N37 Rail: Waverley

11(12.30 Sun) - 1am

Caledonian Deuchars IPA[H]

One room studenty pub with large comfy settees, two TV's and a juke box. Live music six nights a week and a quiz on Sun. evening. Funny poetic quotations and collages all over. Check out the toilets.

BS

Blue Blazer   C7

2 Spittal Street, EH3 9DX

(0131) 229 5030

Bus: Lothian 2 (or 1, 10, 11, 15/15A, 16, 17, 24, 34, 35, N11, N16 to Lothian Road) Rail: Haymarket

11(12.30 Sun) - 1am

Caledonian Deuchars IPA; Cairngorm Trade Winds; Stewart 80/-; 5 Guest Beers[H] ☺

Wood floors and panels, high ceilings and frosted glass windows give this two-room city centre pub a traditional feel, though wee candles along the bar and unobtrusive background music are nice modern touches. It's often busy, but competent staff keep things moving well. Find details of the eight real ales, often from small Scottish breweries, on Facebook (I Love the Blue Blazer). Try the wide range of whiskies, or the monthly rum tasting club for good measure.

BS DW

Bow Bar   G6

80 West Bow, EH1 2HH

(0131) 226 7667

Bus: Lothian 2 (or 23, 27, 41, 42, 45, N27 to George IV Bridge) Rail: Waverley

12 - 11.30; 12.30 - 11 Sun

Belhaven 80/- Ale; Caledonian Deuchars IPA; Taylor Landlord; 5 Guest Beers[A] ☺

A classic Scottish one roomed alehouse dedicated to traditional Scottish air pressure dispense and perpendicular drinking. The five guest beers can be from anywhere in the UK. The walls are festooned with original brewery mirrors and the superb gantry does justice to an award winning selection of single malt whisky. A map of the original 33 Scottish counties hangs above the fire place.

BS (lunchtime)   DW

Braidburn   U8

200 Mayfield Road, EH9 3BE

(0131) 667 3867

Bus: Lothian 7, 31, 37, 47, N31, N47

12(12.30 Sun) - 11(Midnight Fri & Sat)

Caledonian Deuchars IPA[P]

A comfortable lounge bar, focused on food, with a conservatory restaurant. WARNING: Real ale has a very low profile, being hidden on the keg beer dispense taps.

DA   OD   MD (12(12.30 Sun)-9.30)   BS   CW (until 8.30)

Brass Monkey   J6

14 Drummond St., EH8 9TU

(0131) 556 1961

Bus: Lothian 2, 3/3A, 5, 7, 8, 14, 29, 30, 31, 33, 37, 47, X47, X48, 49, N3, N8, N30, N31, N37
Rail: Waverley

11(12.30 Sun) - 1am

Caledonian Deuchars IPA[H] ☺

A small pub split over several rooms, popular with students. Boasts a 20 seat cinema, with a film showing daily at 3pm and evening bookings for private parties.

OD (pavement tables)   BS

Bruntsfield Hotel (Bisque)   S6

69-74 Bruntsfield Place, EH10 4HH

(0131) 229 1393

Bus: Lothian 11, 15/15A, 16, 17, 23, 45, N11, N16

11(12.30 Sun) - 1am

Caledonian Deuchars IPA[P] ☺

Impressive stone built hotel overlooking the Bruntsfield links. The basement café-bar has recently been extensively refurbished. There is an extensive menu, also available in a separate bistro after 5pm.

AC   DA (bell for assistance)   OD (patio/garden)
MD   BS   CW (if eating)

Buckstone Bistro   S8

Braid Hills Hotel, 143 Braid Road, EH10 6JD

(0131) 447 8888

Bus: Lothian 5, 11, 15/15A, 16, N11, N16

11(12 Sun) - 11

Belhaven 80/-; Caledonian Deuchars IPA; Harvieston Bitter & Twisted[H] ☺

Bar and conservatory restaurant built adjacent to the imposing Victorian Braid Hills Hotel. The interior is modern in design with a corrian bar top with brass rails along the bottom. It has a bright feel due to the use of light wood and natural light from the conservatory. Handy for the Braid Hills golf course and walks in the Hermitage of Braid.

AC   DA   OD (scenic patio)   MD (11-9)   BS
(lunchtime)   CW

Burlington Berties   S6

11-13 Tarvit Street, EH3 9AW

(0131) 229 8659

Bus: Lothian 10, 11, 15/15A, 16, 17, 23, 27, 45, N11, N16, N27

11(12 Sun) - 1am

Caledonian Deuchars IPA[H]

The diverse clientele is a mix of locals and thespians from the nearby King's Theatre. Décor includes two large pub mirrors, and numerous theatre posters on the lounge walls. Impressive jukebox and a quiz night every Monday.

BS   CW   DW

Cafe Royal   H2

19 West Register St., EH2 2AA (off E end of Princes St.)

(0131) 556 1884

Bus: City Centre   Rail: Waverley (close) ☺

11(12.30 Sun) - 11(Midnight Thu; 1am Fri & Sat)

Caledonian Deuchars IPA, 80; 2 Guest Beers[H]

One of the finest Victorian pub interiors in Scotland, listed on CAMRA's national pub inventory.

Dominated by an impressive oval island bar with ornate brass light fittings and six magnificent ceramic tiled murals of innovators made by Doulton from pictures by John Eyre. The magnificent sporting windows of the Oyster bar were made by the same Edinburgh firm who supplied windows for the House of Lords. The gents features an unusual hand basin.

MD (until 10)   BS

Caley Sample Room   R6

56 Angle Park Terrace, EH11 2JR

(0131) 337 7204

Bus: Lothian 4, 34, 35, 44, N44

11(10 Sat & Sun) - Midnight(1am Fri & Sat)

Caledonian Deuchars IPA, 80; 2 Guest Beers[H] ☺

Recently refurbished, one-room bar that serves beers from across the UK, and an extensive range of wines, to accompany its interesting and varied menu. Generally relaxed, but the atmosphere hots up when Hearts are at home.

DA   MD (11.30(10 Sat & Sun)-9(10 Fri & Sat))   BS CW (until 8pm)   DW (not in food area)

Cambridge Bar   B2

20 Young Street, EH2 4JB

(0131) 226 2120

Bus: City Centre

12 - 11(Midnight Thu; 1am Fri & Sat)

Caledonian Deuchars IPA, Guest Beer[H] ☺

New Town bar with single L-shaped room and comfortable 3 piece suite in front of the bar. The gourmet burgers provide an excellent alternative to the well known fast food(?) outlets, but expect a longer preparation time.

DA (rear door)   MD (12-9)   BS   CW (until 5pm)

Cameo Bar   U2

23 Commercial Street, EH6 6JA

(0131) 554 9999

Bus: Lothian 16, 22, 35, 36, N22

12(12.30 Sun) - 1am

Greene King IPA[H] ☺

Spacious, multi-level, cafe bar style pub with a variety of seating. Impressive bar counter panel and metal sculptures feature inside and out. Sunday is

quiz night, free Wi-Fi access and plenty of screens showing main sports events.

MD (12-9)   BS

Canon's Gait   U5

232 Canongate, EH8 8DQ

(0131) 556 4481

Bus: Lothian 35, 36   Rail: Waverley

12(12.30 Sun) - 11(Midnight Fri & Sat)

Beer Range (2) Varies[H] ☺

Situated on the historic Royal Mile this bar is on two levels. At street level there is a comfortable lounge bar. Downstairs is a stone floored bar used for functions, occasional ceilidhs and open mike sessions on Thu.

ML (12-3; not Sun)

Cask and Barrel   T4

115 Broughton Street, EH1 3RZ

(0131) 556 3132

Bus: Lothian 8, 13, 17, N8   Rail: Waverley

11(12.30 Sun) - 12.30am(1am Thu-Sat)

Draught Bass; Caledonian Deuchars IPA, 80; Hadrian & Border Cowie; Harvieston Bitter & Twisted; 4 Guest Beers[H] ☺

Spacious and busy alehouse drawing a varied clientele of all ages, ranging from business people to football fans. The interior features an imposing horseshoe bar, bare floorboards, a splendid cornice and a collection of brewery mirrors. Old barrels act as tables for those who wish to stand up, or cannot find a seat. The guest beers, often from smaller Scottish breweries, feature a range of strengths and styles. Sparklers removed on request.

DA   OD (pavement tables)   ML   BS

Castle Arms   G5

6 Johnstone Terrace, EH1 2PW

(0131) 225 7432

Bus: Lothian 2 Grassmarket (or 23, 27, 41, 42, 45, N27 to George IV Bridge)   Rail: Waverley

11(12.30 Sun) - 11(1am Fri & Sat)

Caledonian Deuchars IPA, 80; 3 Guest Beers[H] ☺

Built on the hill-side close to the castle, this bistro style bar occupies several levels of a building typical of Edinburgh's old town. The main, seemingly ground level entrance, leads into a pleasant plainly furnished bar with wooden floor. There is also a small snug. Stairs descend to another bar which has access to terrace with superb views over the Grassmarket below.

DA   OD (terrace)   MD (11-10)   BS   CW (until 8pm)

Centre Court   Q8

124 Colinton Road, EH14 1BY

(0131) 443 9867

Bus: Lothian 10, 27, 45, N27   Rail: Slateford

11 - Midnight(1am Fri & Sat)

Caledonian Deuchars IPA[H]

One roomed traditionally styled semi-circular bar due for refurbishment in Jun 08. Very friendly and comfortable. Tennis courts over the road if you want to work off the beer.

OD (tables at front)   MD (12-8)   BS   CW

Chanter   C7

30-32 Bread Street, EH3 9AF

(0131) 211 0575

Bus: Lothian 2 (or 1, 10, 11, 15/15A, 16, 17, 24, 34, 35, N11, N16 to Lothian Road)   Rail: Haymarket

11(12.30 Sun) - 1am

Caledonian Deuchars IPA, 80; 3 Guest Beers[H]

Former Hogshead, now a busy outlet with varied seating areas. Offers many TV screens for sports, 2 pool tables and games machines. A Nintendo Wii available for hire with games nights. Quizzes and student discount nights Sun & Wed.

DA   MD (11(12.30 Sun)-10)   BS

Clarks Bar   S4

142 Dundas Street, EH3 5DQ

(0131) 556 1067

Bus: Lothian 23, 27, 36

11(12.30 Sun) - 11(11.30 Thu-Sat)

Caledonian Deuchars IPA[P], 80[H]; Guest Beer[P] ☺

Basic tenement bar popular with the locals and workers from the many offices nearby. The internal layout is interesting with 2 private rooms off the bar. Several brewery mirrors and some photos from the days when trams ran outside adorn the main room.

The steep stairs make a trip to the toilets a good test of sobriety. Don't miss the interesting mural on the way.

ML   BS   DW

Cloisters Bar   S6

26 Brougham Street, EH3 9JH

(0131) 221 9997

Bus: Lothian 24 (or 10, 11, 15/15A, 16, 17, 23, 27, 45, N11, N16, N27 to Tollcross)

12(12.30 Sun) - Midnight(1am Fri & Sat)

Caledonian Deuchars IPA; Cairngorm Trade Winds; Stewart Holy Grale; Taylor Landlord; 5 Guest Beers[H] ☺

A former parsonage, this bare boarded alehouse is popular with a broad cross section of drinkers. Large bench seats give the pub a friendly feel. A fine selection of brewery mirrors adorn the walls and the wide range of single malt whiskies does justice to the outstanding gantry, which is built using wood from a redundant church. A spiral staircase makes visiting the loo an adventure. No TV.

ML (12-4; 3 Mon)   ME (6-8.30 Tue-Thu)   MD (12-6 Fri & Sat)   BS   DW

Club Room   G2

14 George Street, EH2 2PF (by Dome entrance)

(0131) 624 8626

Bus: City Centre   Rail: Waverley

10 - 5(11 Thu-Sat); Closed Sun

Caledonian Deuchars IPA[P] ☺

Same entrance as the Dome, but turn left after the revolving door. A high ceilinged bar with recently created, but superb, 1930's art deco interior is more of a tea-room than a bar by day.

DA (bell for assistance)   MD   CW

Colinton Inn   O10

12-14 Bridge Road, EH13 0LQ

(0131) 441 3218

Bus: Lothian 10, 16, 18, 45, N16

11(12.30 Sun) - Midnight(1am Fri; 12.30am Sat)

Caledonian Deuchars IPA; Greene King Old Speckled Hen[P] ☺

Comfortable locals' L shaped lounge bar, often busy but orderly. The bar, which has a wooden gantry, is at one side and seating at the other. Down-stairs is a large function suite.

DA   OD (garden)   ML (1-3.30 Sun)   CW (until 6pm)

Conan Doyle   T5

73 York Place, EH1 3JD

(0131) 557 9539

Bus: Lothian 1, 4, 5, 7, 8, 10, 11, 12, 14, 15/15A, 16, 17, 19, 22, 25, 26, 34, 44/44A, 45, 49, N3, N8, N11, N16, N22, N25, N26, N37, N44   Rail: Waverley

12(12.30 Sun) - Midnight(1am Fri & Sat)

Caledonian Deuchars IPA, 80[H]

Sherlock Holmes themed bar, on a busy corner, with some historical displays. Chill-out music predominates at the weekend. Handy for the Playhouse and St. James shopping centre.

OD (pavement tables)   MD (12-9(8 Fri-Sun))

Cooper's   I3

Waverley Station, EH1 1BB

(0131) 557 9124

Bus: City Centre   Rail: Waverley (close)

7am(12.30 Sun) - 11(Midnight Fri & Sat)

Greene King IPA; Fullers London Pride[H]

Lounge-style bar off listed station waiting hall. Possibly the only mainline station bar in Scotland selling real ale. Note the early opening time and food availability.

DA   ML (7(10 Sun)-3)   BS

Corstorphine Inn   N6

17 Corstorphine High St., EH12 7SU

(0131) 334 1019

Bus: Lothian 1

11 - Midnight; 12.30 - 1am Sun

Caledonian Deuchars IPA; Inveralmond Ossian; Guest Beer[H]   ☺

Suburban village local with separate dining area. Wide variety of customers. Monday night is quiz night. The large screen TV is popular for sporting events.

DA   MD   CW

Cozi Bar & Grill   S4

44 St. Stephen St., EH3 5AL

(0131) 220 1233

Bus: Lothian 24, 29, 36, 42

5(12 Fri; 11 Sat; 12.30 Sun) - 11(Midnight Wed & Thu; 1am Fri & Sat; 9 Sun)

Guest Beer[H]

Light, spacious, New Town, cellar bar with wooden floors. Art work adorns the walls and a general sense of good taste prevails. The guest beer is usually from Inveralmond.

ML (12-2.30 Fri)   ME (5-9)   MD (11-9 Sat; 11-7.30 Sun)   DW (bar only)

Cumberland Bar   T4

1-3 Cumberland Street, EH3 6RT

(0131) 558 3134

Bus: Lothian 14, 23, 27

11(12.30 Sun) - 1am

Caledonian Deuchars IPA, 80; Taylor Landlord; 5 Guest Beers[H]   ☺

Elegant but traditional New Town pub with half wood panelling. Exquisite, large, ornate brewery mirrors hang beside framed, decorative and illustrative posters. The wood finish is enhanced by dark green leather seating. There are two drinking areas linked by a wide corridor where people stand when it's busy.

DA   OD (garden & patio)   ML (12-2.30)   ME (5-9)   BS   CW (rear room during day)   DW (cats also)

Dagda Bar   U6

93-95 Buccleuch St., EH8 9NG

(0131) 667 9773

Bus: Lothian 41, 42   Rail: Waverley

12(11 Sat; 12.30 Sun) - 1am

Beer Range (3) Varies   ☺

Convivial, cosy bar in university area attracting a wide ranging clientele. The single room has banquette seating on 3 sides and the bar counter on the other. The stone flagged floor is a little uneven in places. The staff are happy to let you sample the 3 real ales, which are usually from smaller breweries. Fresh ground coffee and quality tea also available.

DW

Dalriada – CAMRA 2008 Edinburgh Pub of the Year runner up

Dalriada   Z5

77 Promenade, EH15 2EL

(0131) 454 4500

Bus: Lothian 15/15A, 26, N26

12 - 11(Midnight Fri & Sat); Closed Mon in Jan & Feb

Beer Range (3) Varies[H] ☺

Located on the Portobello/Joppa promenade, you can enjoy a pint and watch out for seals! The imposing entrance of this stone built villa has an original tiled floor and fireplace. There are 3 bar areas with wooden flooring and furniture. The bar counter has a polished Italian granite top. An extensive snack menu is available 12-3 (not Mon). Live music at weekends. CAMRA 2008 Edinburgh Pub of the Year runner up.

OD BS CW (until 8pm) DW (on lead - dog bowls provided)

Deacon Brodies Tavern   G5

435 Lawnmarket, EH1 2NT

(0131) 255 6531

Bus: Lothian 23, 27, 41, 42, 45, N27 Rail: Waverley

10am - 11(1.30am Fri & Sat)

Caledonian Deuchars IPA[A] ☺

Busy, loud, traditional, High Street pub and restaurant. Popular with locals and tourists. Take time to look at the ceiling.

DA MD (10-9.45) CW (until 5pm (8pm in restaurant))

Dell Inn   P8

27 Lanark Road, EH14 1TG

(0131) 443 9991

Bus: Lothian 4, 20, 34, 44/44A, N44 Rail: Slateford

11(12.30 Sun) - 11

Caledonian Deuchars IPA; Guest Beer[H]

Large L-shaped lounge area, raised one end, with recently refurbished décor. Nice gantry, friendly staff, and good food. Outdoor area with lovely outlook over the Water of Leith.

DA OD MD (11(12.30 Sun)-9(10 Fri-Sun)) CW

Dirty Dicks C3

159 Rose Street, EH2 4LS

(0131) 225 4610

Bus: City Centre

11 - 11(1am Fri & Sat)

Caledonian Deuchars IPA; Guest Beer[H] ☺

Bar cum bistro with dark, stone walled interior. Decor has a Swiss/German feel with a stone floor and wooden ceiling. Music can be loud in evenings.

OD (pavement tables) MD (11-10) CW (until 9pm)

Doctors H7

32 Forrest Road, EH1 2QN

(0131) 225 1819

Bus: Lothian 2, 23, 27, 35, 41, 42, 45, N27 Rail: Waverley

11(12.30) - Midnight(1am Fri & Sat)

Caledonian Deuchars IPA, 80; Courage Directors; 5 Guest Beers[H] ☺

Large wooden floored, L shaped bar. Adjacent to Edinburgh University's Medical School so is popular with students. The guest beers are generally from smaller Scottish Breweries.

OD (pavement tables) MD (11-10) BS CW (until 8pm, if over 14)

Dome G2

14 George Street, EH2 2PF

(0131) 624 8624

Bus: City Centre Rail: Waverley

9am - 11(Midnight Thu; 1am Fri & Sat)

Caledonian Deuchars IPA[P]

Straight through the chequered floored entrance hall is the magnificent domed ceilinged restaurant bar. This bright airy ornate bar offers an excellent menu in very swish surroundings.

DA (bell for assistance) OD (garden cafe) MD BS CW

Doric Bar H4

15-16 Market Street, EH1 1DE

(0131) 225 5243

Bus: 36, Airlink 100 (or City Centre) Rail: Waverley (close)

11.30 - 11.30(1am Fri & Sat)

Caledonian Deuchars IPA[P]

Wooden floored bar with corniced ceiling. A large Lorimer and Clarks mirror decorates the bare stone walls. Real ale also available in the upstairs restaurant.

ML ME (restaurant only) BS CW (until 4pm downstairs, 8pm upstairs)

Drouthy Neebors U6

1 West Preston Street, EH8 9PX

(0131) 662 9617

Bus: Lothian 42 (or 3/3A, 5, 7, 30, 31, 33, 37, 47, 49, N3, N8, N30, N31, N37 to South Clerk St)

11(12.30 Sun) - 1am

Belhaven 80/-; Greene King IPA[H]

Recently refurbished, with various Edinburgh prints decorating the walls. Fairly quiet, despite the five TV screens. Good selection of bottled Belgian beers available. Popular with students and locals.

BS

Dunstane House Hotel R5

4 West Coats, EH12 5JQ

(0131) 337 6169

Bus: Lothian 12, 26, 31, N26 Rail: Haymarket

12 - 11

Orkney Dark Island[H]

The Stane Bar has a small wood panelled area adjacent to the bar, next to a larger room with armchairs and picture window overlooking the front garden, both decorated with period photos. Impressive selection of malt whiskies.

AC OD (garden) ML (12-2) ME (5.30-9.30) MD (12-9.30 Sat & Sun) BS CW

Element D3

110-114 Rose St, EH2 3JF

(0131) 225 3297

Bus: City Centre Rail: Waverley

11(12.30 Sun) - 1am

Caledonian Deuchars IPA[P]

Recently fitted open plan gastro pub style bar with very nice modern gantry. Very comfortable high tables & stools predominate.

OD (pavement couches) MD (11-10) CW (until 8pm)

The Scottish Borders

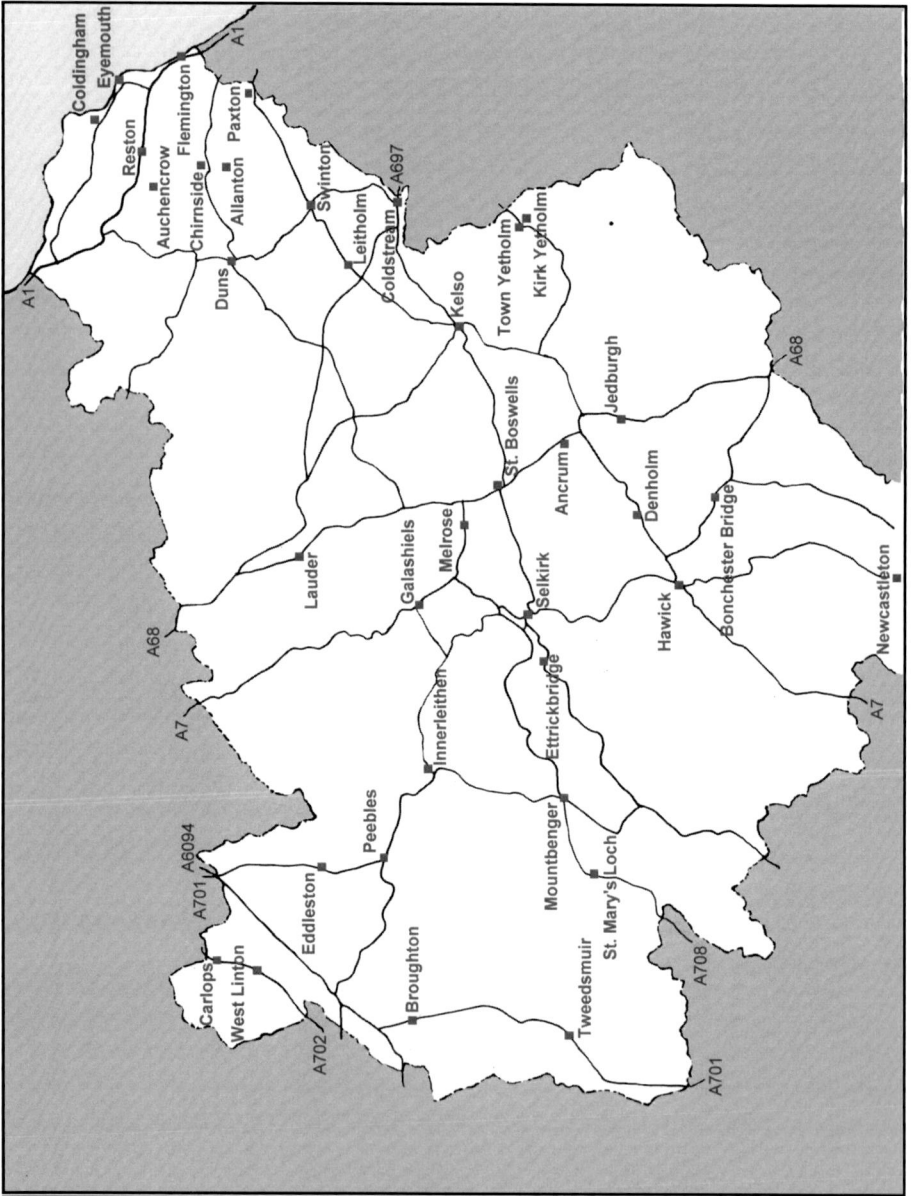

The Lothians

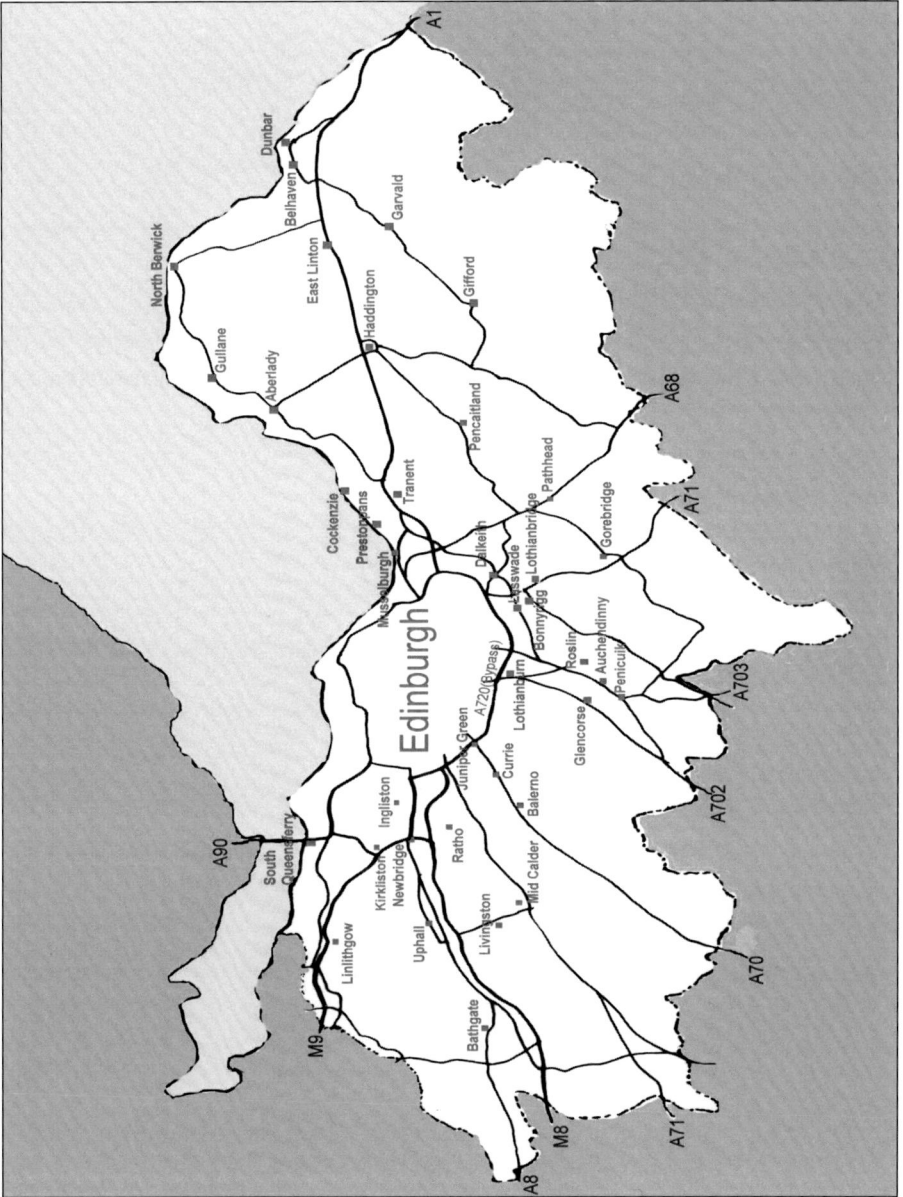

Outer Edinburgh

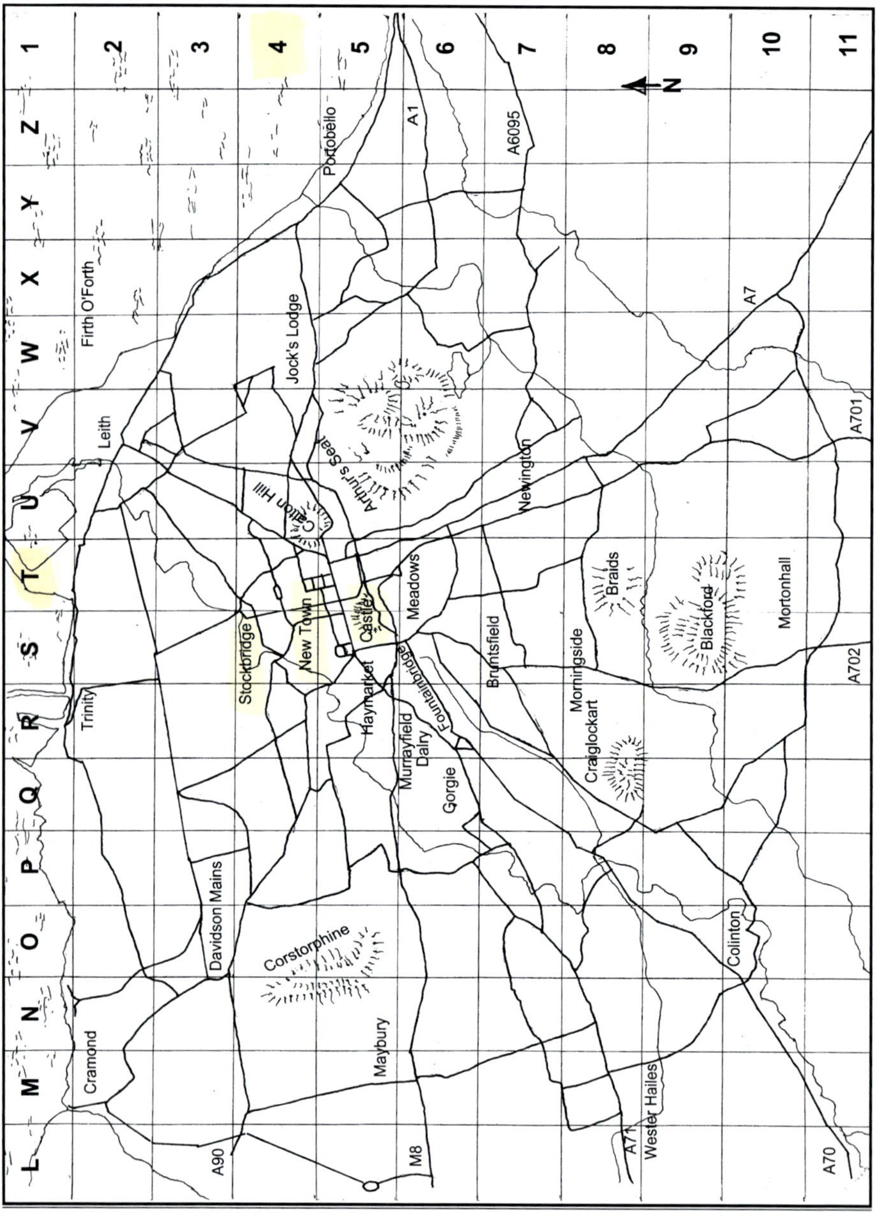

Map grid reference columns: L M N O P Q R S T U V W X Y Z
Map grid reference rows: 1 2 3 4 5 6 7 8 9 10 11

N

Firth O'Forth

Portobello · A1 · A6095 · A7 · A701

Jock's Lodge

Leith

Calton Hill · Arthur's Seat

Newington

Braids · Blackford · Mortonhall

Stockbridge · New Town · Castle · Meadows · Bruntsfield · Morningside · Craiglockart · A702

Trinity · Haymarket · Fountainbridge · Murrayfield · Dairy · Gorgie

Davidson Mains · Colinton

Corstorphine

Cramond · Maybury · Wester Hailes

A90 · M8 · A71 · A70

Inner Edinburgh

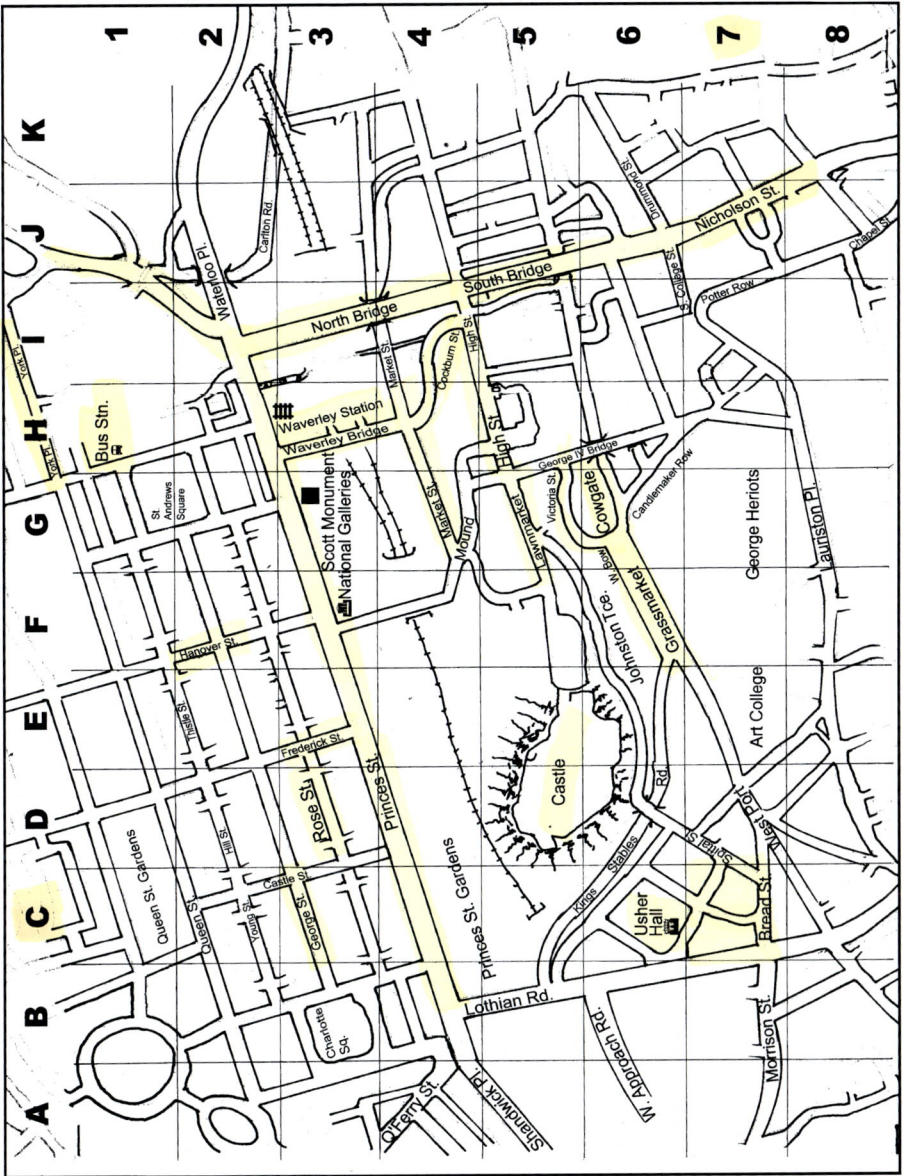

Edinburgh Pubs By Grid Reference

A3	Indigo Yard	I5	Advocate	S6	Bennets Bar
A4	H P Mathers	I7	Teviot Row	S6	Bruntsfield Hotel
A5	Au Bar	J4	Bank Hotel	S6	Burlington Berties
A5	Grosvenor	J4	Mitre	S6	Cloisters Bar
B2	Cambridge Bar	J5	Bannermans	S6	Illicit Still
B4	Ryan's Bar	J5	Whistle Binkies	S6	International Bar
B4	Whighams Wine Bar	J6	Brass Monkey	S6	Links Hotel
B6	Shakespeare	J6	Royal Oak	S7	Golf Tavern
B7	Festival Tavern	J8	56 North	S7	Montpeliers
B7	Filmhouse	J8	Peartree House	S7	Morningside Glory
B8	Banter	K4	Tass	S7	Waiting Room
C2	Oxford Bar	K4	Tolbooth Tavern	S8	Bennet's Bar
C3	Dirty Dicks	K4	World's End	S8	Buckstone Bistro
C3	Hogshead	K8	Southsider	T1	Starbank Inn
C3	Rose & Crown	N6	Corstorphine Inn	T2	Victoria Park Hotel
C3	Scott's Bar	N6	Winston's	T3	Blind Beggar
C7	Blue Blazer	O10	Colinton Inn	T4	Barony Bar
C7	Chanter	O10	Spylaw Tavern	T4	Cask and Barrel
D2	Queens Arms	O3	Lauriston Farm	T4	Cumberland Bar
D3	Element	O3	Olde Inn	T4	Lloyds No 1
D3	Kenilworth	O6	Struan Hotel	T4	Orchard
D7	Footlights	P8	Dell Inn	T4	Phoenix
E2	Standing Order	Q5	Hampton Hotel	T4	Smithies Ale House
E2	Thistle St. Bar	Q6	Station Tavern	T4	Star Bar
E2	World	Q8	Centre Court	T4	Wally Dug
E3	Black Rose	R10	Hunter's Tryst	T4	Wm Mather & Son
E3	Great Grog	R5	Dunstane House Hotel	T5	Conan Doyle
E3	Rose St. Brewery	R5	Haymarket Bar	U11	Stable Bar
F1	Jam House	R5	Menzies Belford Hotel	U2	Cameo Bar
F2	99 Hanover St.	R5	Mercat	U2	Old Dock Bar
F2	Milnes	R5	Roseburn Bar	U2	Roseleaf
F6	Beehive Inn (Drones)	R5	Ryries	U2	Rumba
F6	Black Bull	R6	Athletic Arms (Diggers)	U2	Teuchter's Landing
F6	Last Drop Tavern	R6	Caley Sample Room	U2	Village Inn
F6	White Hart Inn	R6	Golden Rule	U3	Foot O' T' Walk
G2	Abbotsford	R6	McCowan's Brewhouse	U3	Robbies Bar
G2	Club Room	R7	Royal Ettrick Hotel	U4	Artisan
G2	Dome	S1	Harbour Inn	U4	Pearce's
G5	Castle Arms	S1	Old Chain Pier	U4	Theatre Royal
G5	Deacon Brodies Tavern	S10	Mortenhall Golf Club	U4	Windsor Buffet
G5	Ensign Ewart	S10	Pavilion	U5	Canon's Gait
G5	Jolly Judge	S2	Peacock Inn	U6	Abbey Bar
G6	Bow Bar	S4	Antiquary	U6	Auld Hoose
H2	Cafe Royal	S4	Baillie	U6	Blind Poet
H2	Guildford Arms	S4	Bert's Bar	U6	Dagda Bar
H2	Tiles Bistro Bar	S4	Clarks Bar	U6	Drouthy Neebors
H4	Doric Bar	S4	Cozi Bar & Grill	U6	Maltings Ale House
H4	Hebrides Bar	S4	Hamiltons Bar & Kitchen	U6	Meadow Bar
H4	Malt Shovel Inn	S4	Hector's	U6	Reverie
H5	Villager	S4	Iglu	U6	Wm McEwans Alehouse
H6	Greyfriars Bobby Bar	S4	Kay's Bar	U7	Leslies Bar
H7	Doctors	S4	St. Vincent Bar	U7	Minders
H7	Sandy Bells	S4	Standard	U7	Old Bell
I3	Cooper's	S5	Bert's Bar	U8	Braidburn
I4	Albanach	S5	Melville Lounge	V2	Granary
I4	Halfway House	S5	Scruffy Murphy's	V2	Harry Hall's Carrier's Qu'
I4	Jinglin Geordies	S5	Teuchters	V2	Kings Wark
I4	Royal McGregor	S5	Thomson's	V2	Malt and Hops
I4	Scotsman Lounge	S6	Auld Toll		

Ellwyn Hotel   W4

37-39 Moira Terrace, EH7 6TD

(0131) 669 1033

Bus: Lothian 12 Kings Road, 21 Royal Inf, 15/15A, 26, N26

11 - Midnight; 12.30 - 11 Sun

Guest Beer[P]

Comfortable hotel lounge bar on the way to Edinburgh's seaside suburb of Portobello. The beer is often from either Harviestoun or Stewart's.

AC OD (garden to rear) ML ME (residents only) BS DW

Ensign Ewart   G5

521 Lawnmarket, EH1 2PE

(0131) 225 7440

Bus: Lothian 23, 27, 35, 41, 42, 45, N27 Rail: Waverley

11(12.30Sun) - 11

Caledonian Deuchars IPA, 80, XPA[H] ☺

Interesting 2 roomed pub, dating from 1690, with traditional military theme. Being very close to the castle it is very popular with tourists, but as a result it is not one of Edinburgh's cheaper pubs.

MD BS

Festival Tavern   B7

18 Morrison Street, EH10 7BJ

(0131) 222 9000

Bus: Lothian 1, 2, 10, 11, 15/15A, 16, 17, 24, 34, N11, N16 Rail: Haymarket

11(12.30 Sun) - Midnight(1am Fri & Sat)

Caledonian Deuchars IPA[H]

Large single roomed bare boarded bar handy for theatres, cinemas, restaurants and the EICC. Occasional live music. Outdoor drinking spoilt by the traffic.

OD (terrace at front) MD (11-9(6 Mon; 5 Fri-Sun)) BS

Filmhouse   B7

88 Lothian Road, EH3 9BZ

(0131) 229 5932

Bus: Lothian 1, 10, 11, 15/15A, 16, 17, 24, 34, N11, N16, N22, N30 Rail: Haymarket

10 - 11.30(12.30am Fri & Sat); 12.30 - 10 Sun

Stewart Pentland IPA; Orkney Dark Island; 2 Guest Beers[H] ☺

A cafe style bar in specialist cinema. One end of the bar dispenses the real ales. The other is where food and coffee can be purchased. The guest ales are often from Arran or Inveralmond. Good quality café style food is served all day, with options for vegetarians and vegans. Not the cheapest bar in town, but it attracts many customers other than the cinema goers. The Usher Hall and the Lyceum and Traverse theatres are 5 minutes walk away.

DA MD (10-10) CW (10-8)

Foot O' T' Walk   U3

183 Constitution St., EH6 7AA

(0131) 553 0120

Bus: Lothian 1, 7, 10, 12, 14, 16, 21, 22, 25, 34, 35, 36, 49, N22, N25

9(12.30 Sun) - 11(Midnight Thu-Sat)

Caledonian Deuchars IPA, 80; Greene King Abbot; 4 Guest Beers; Weston's Cider[H] ☺

A JD Wetherspoon's pub which attracts a large cultural cross-section of Leith's denizens. Reasonably priced food is served in a seemingly low ceilinged but spacious room broken into discrete eating areas by the trade-mark dias in one corner and waist high brass railinged wood panels. It's corner location affords two main entrances, and a third door to Constitution St.

DA MD (9-11) BS CW (until 8pm)

Footlights   D7

7-11 Spittal Street, EH3 9DY

(0131) 229 6466

Bus: Lothian 2 (or 1, 10, 11, 15/15A, 16, 17, 24, 34, 35, N11, N16 to Lothian Road) Rail: Haymarket

11(12.30 Sun) - 1am

Caledonian Deuchars IPA[H]

One room bar on two levels, with a wooden floor. A pool table, two bandits, a quiz machine, 5 TV's and a large screen provide the entertainment.

OD (pavement tables) MD (11-10) BS CW (if eating)

Golden Rule   R6

30 Yeaman Place, EH11 1BU

(0131) 229 3413

Bus: Lothian 1, 10, 23, 27, 34, 35   Rail: Haymarket

12(11 Sat) - Midnight; 12.30 - 11.00 Sun

Caledonian Deuchars IPA; Harviestoun Bitter & Twisted; 2 Guest Beers[H] ☺

Split-level, locals' bar in a Victorian tenement. The two guest beers are usually from smaller breweries. The downstairs bar caters more for the trendier end of the market.

BS

Golf Tavern   S7

31 Wrights Houses, EH10 4HR

(0131) 221 5221

Bus: Lothian 11, 15/15A, 16, 17, 23, 45, N11, N16

12(11 Sun) - 1am

Caledonian Deuchars IPA[P]

One of Edinburgh's oldest taverns (est. 1456), now a sports bar. No trace of the original except for the outside. Contains Scotland's largest collection of golf memorabilia and adjacent to the worlds oldest short hole (36) golf course.

OD (quiet pavement tables) MD (until 10) BS CW (until 8pm, if eating)

Granary   V2

32-34 Shore, EH6 6QN

(0845) 166 6005

Bus: Lothian 16, 22, 35, 36, N22

11(10 Sat & Sun) - 1am

Caledonian Deuchars IPA[P]

Large L shaped restaurant/bar with function suite upstairs. Comfortable plush seating throughout. Live pianist on Fri/Sat evenings and Sun lunch.

DA OD (pavement tables) MD (12-10) CW

Great Grog   E3

43 Rose St., EH2 2NH

(0131) 225 1616

Bus: City Centre Rail: Waverley

10 - 11(Midnight Fri & Sat)

Cairngorm Trade Winds[H]

Wine bar on two levels with an exceptionally well-stocked cellar. Upstairs is a comfy lounge area, downstairs and outside the décor is clean and modern in a café style. "Bar snacks" are of a superior quality.

DA (via hotel next door) OD (pavement tables) BS CW (until 7pm)

Greyfriars Bobby Bar   H6

34 Candlemaker Row, EH1 2QE

(0131) 225 8328

Bus: Lothian 2, 23, 27, 35, 41, 42, 45, N27 Rail: Waverley

12 - Midnight(1am Sat); 12.30 - 1am Sun

Caledonian Deuchars IPA, 80[H] ☺

Dating from 1893, a split level, long bar named after Edinburgh's famous "wee dug", whose statue sits outside. The walls are decorated with pictures of Edinburgh, its' people and the "wee dug".

MD (until 9) BS CW (until 8pm)

Grosvenor   A5

26-28 Shandwick Place, EH2 4RT

(0131) 226 4579

Bus: City Centre Rail: Haymarket.

12 - Midnight(1am Fri & Sat)

Beer Range (2) Varies[H]

Modernised lounge with interesting gothic-style bar which is "listed". Popular for food at lunchtimes and evenings, with patio doors opening onto the street. Real ale usually from Kelburn.

MD (12-9) BS

Guildford Arms   H2

1 West Register Street, EH2 2AA (off E end of Princes St.)

(0131) 556 4312

Bus: City Centre Rail: Waverley (close)

11(12.30 Sun) - 11(Midnight Fri & Sat)   ☺

Caledonian Deuchars IPA, XPA[P]; Orkney Dark Island; Stewart Pentland IPA; 7 Guest Beers[H]

Busy, but orderly, city centre pub. The high ceiling, cornices and friezes are spectacular, as are the window arches and screens. An unusual gallery above the main bar, where the restaurant is located, is

also noteworthy. There are areas for standing and others with seating. The diverse guest beer range often features smaller breweries. Piped music can be a little loud at times.

ML (12-2.30) ME (6-9.30) BS

H P Mathers   (QS]   A4

1 Queensferry Street, EH2 4PA

(0131) 225 3549

Bus: City Centre   Rail: Haymarket

11 - Midnight (1am Fri & Sat); 12.30 - 11 Sun

Caledonian Deuchars IPA; Caledonian 80; 4 Guest Beers[H] ☺

A genuine, busy, traditional, Scottish single roomed, stand up drinking shop. Features are a wooden floor, a high ceiling with ornate plasterwork below the cornice, big stained glass windows, large dark wood bar fittings and an excellent collection of rare brewery mirrors.

BS

Halfway House   I4

24 Fleshmarket Close, EH1 1BX (up steps opposite station's Market St. entrance)

(0131) 225 7101

Bus: Lothian 36 to E. Market St (or 3/3A, 5, 7, 8, 14, 29, 30, 31, 33, 35, 37, 47, X47, X48, 49, N3, N8, N30, N31, N37 to Tron) Rail: Waverley (close)

11(12.30 Sun) - Midnight(1am Fri & Sat)

4 Guest Beers[H] ☺

Cosy, characterful bar hidden halfway down an old town "close". Railway memorabilia and current timetables adorn the interior of this small, often busy, bar. Usually there are 4 interesting beers from smaller Scottish breweries. Over the summer a different brewery is showcased each week. CAMRA members (show card) get a discount on their first pint. Good quality, reasonably priced food. May open until 1am at busy times of the year.

OD (pavement tables) MD BS CW DW

Hamiltons Bar & Kitchen   S4

16-18 Hamilton Place, EH3 5AU

(0131) 226 4199

Bus: Lothian 24, 29, 36, 42

11.30(11 Sat; 12.30 Sun) - Midnight(1am Thu-Sat); Closed Mon

Caledonian Deuchars IPA[P]

Large wooden floored bar, popular with New Town locals. Although open, plan pillars divide the space into several areas. Sofas provide comfortable seating.

DA   ML (12-2.30; 11-4 Sat & Sun)   ME (6(5 Sun)-10)   BS   CW (until 8pm)   DW

Hampton Hotel   Q5

14 Corstorphine Road, EH12 6HN

(0131) 337 1130

Bus: Lothian 12, 26, 31, X48, N26, N31

11(12.30 Sun) - Midnight(1am Fri & Sat)

Caledonian Deuchars IPA; Guest Beer[H]

Comfortable lounge bar and restaurant with sporting memorabilia, ornate cornices and chandeliers in a large villa. Close to Murryfield rugby stadium. TV's show sport, but no piped music.

AC OD (garden) ML (12-3) ME (5.30-9) BS CW (in restaurant) DW

Harbour Inn   S1

4-6 Fishmarket Square, EH6 4LW

(0131) 552 3968

Bus: Lothian 7, 10, 11, 16, N11

11 - Midnight; 12.30 - 11 Sun

Caledonian Deuchars IPA; Greene King IPA; Guest Beer[H]

Historical photographs on the walls and sea-charts on the ceiling decorate this small traditional pub. A local pub with clientele of all ages. Live music every Sat. evening. Bar snacks only in summer.

OD (pavement tables) BS DW

Harry Hall's Carrier's Quarters   V2

42 Bernard Street, EH6 6PR

(0131) 554 4122

Bus: Lothian 16, 22, 35, 36, N22

12(12.30 Sun) - 1am

Caledonian Deuchars IPA; Guest Beer[H] ☺

Interesting small front bar, where white paintwork gives a bright contrast to the dark floor. A tiny snug cum alcove leads off. A narrow corridor leads to a larger room to rear with stone walls and fire place with inset gas fire.

OD (pavement tables) BS DW

Haymarket Bar R5

11-14 West Maitland St., EH12 5DS

(0131) 228 2537

Bus: Lothian 2, 3/3A, 4, 12, 25, 26, 31, 44/44A, X48, N3, N25, N26, N44 Rail: Haymarket (close)

12(11 Thu & Fri; 12.30 Sun) - Midnight(1am Thu-Sat)

Caledonian Deuchars IPA, 80; Guest Beer(Occasional)[H] ☺

Large, rambling lounge with island bar, raised seating area, balcony and alcove. Often very busy and noisy with several TVs and projection screens showing sport.

DA MD (until 9) BS

Hebrides Bar H4

17 Market Street, EH1 1DE

(0131) 220 4213

Bus: Lothian 36, Airlink 100, (or City Centre) Rail: Waverley (close)

11 - 11(1am Thu-Sat); 12.30 - Midnight Sun

Caledonian Deuchars IPA; Morlands Old Speckled Hen ☺

Small, single-roomed, traditional pub. An impressive Mackays brewery mirror and a map of the Hebrides adorn the dark wood panelled walls.

BS

Hector's S4

47-49 Deanhaugh St., EH4 1LR

(0131) 343 1735

Bus: Lothian 24, 29, 36, 42

12 - Midnight(1am Thu-Sat)

Caledonian Deuchars IPA, Charles Wells Bombardier; Taylor Landlord[H]

The shabby chic décor with dark colour scheme with low light ambiance, including candles on tables, gives this open plan design more of a coffee house feel.

DA ML (12-3(4 weekends)) ME (6-10; not weekends) BS DW

Hogshead C3

22-26 Castle St., EH2 4LS

(0131) 226 1224

Bus: City Centre Rail: Waverley

11(12.30 Sun) - Midnight(1am Fri & Sat)

Caledonian Deuchars IPA, 80; 2 Guest Beers[H]

Large, popular cellar bar with quizzes, 3 large screens for sport and live music on Fridays. Guest beers are usually from Inveralmond.

OD (patio tables) MD (11-10) BS

Hunter's Tryst R10

97 Oxgangs Road, EH13 9NG

(0131) 445 1797

Bus: Lothian 4, 16, 18, 27, N16, N27

12(12.30 Sun) - 11(Midnight Fri & Sat)

Caledonian Deuchars IPA, 80; Greene King Old Speckled Hen; 3 Guest Beer[H] ☺

Pleasant bar converted from farm cottages, with raised extension to the rear and close to Robert Louis Stevenson's childhood home at Swanston. Food orientated, however there is a sizeable area for non-dining drinkers. Beer festivals are held throughout the year, adding to the choice of ales.

DA OD (garden) MD (until 9) BS

Iglu S4

2B Jamaica Street, EH3 6HH

(0131) 476 5333

Bus: Lothian 24, 29, 42

12 - 1am

Weston's Traditional Draught Scrumpy[H]

Café bar with attractive décor, a wooden floor, an exposed stone wall and bench seating. Upstairs is a restaurant. May sell real ale in the near future in addition to the real cider.

ML ME BS DW

Illicit Still S6

2 Brougham Place, EH3 9JH

(0131) 229 4604

Bus: Lothian 10, 11, 15/15A, 16, 17, 23, 24, 27, 45, N11, N16, N27

11(12.30 Sun) - 1am

Caledonian Deuchars IPA, 80[H]

Recently refurbished lounge bar, with modern welcoming feel. Large-screen TV and also a jukebox providing background music.

OD (pavement tables) BS DW

Indigo Yard

A3

Charlotte Lane, EH2 4QZ (off Queensferry St.)

(0131) 220 5603

Bus: City Centre   Rail: Haymarket

11 - 1am

Caledonian Deuchars IPA[P] ☺

Contemporary bistro bar with a mix of different areas including a mezzanine and courtyard. Popular for meals including breakfast.

DA   OD (courtyard)   MD (8.30am-10)   BS   CW (until 6pm)   DW (courtyard only)

International Bar

S6

15 Brougham Place, EH3 9JX

(0131) 229 6815

Bus: Lothian 24 (or 10, 11, 15/15A, 16, 17, 23, 27, 45, N11, N16, N27 to Tollcross)

9am(12.30 Sun) - 1am

Caledonian Deuchars IPA[A]

A mid 19th century locals' bar with lovely stained glass window at the end of the bar. Entertainment provided by two TVs, a bandit, jukebox, Nintendo Wii game system and a big screen. HQ of universities Celtic supporters club.

DA   OD (pavement tables)   BS   DW

Jam House

F1

5 Queen St., EH2 1JE

(0131) 226 4380

Bus: City Centre   Rail: Waverley

6(7.30 Sun) - 1am(3am Fri & Sat); Closed Mon & Tue

Caledonian Deuchars IPA[P]

Former BBC building is now an upmarket music venue with dining in gallery restaurant. WARNING: Admission charges may apply and some events are ticketed.

DA   ME (6-9.30)

Jinglin Geordies

I4

22 Fleshmarket Close, EH1 1BX (up steps opposite station's Market St. entrance)

(0131) 225 2803

Bus: Lothian 36, Airlink 100 (or 3/3A, 5, 7, 8, 14, 29, 30, 31, 33, 35, 37, 47, X47, X48, 49, N3, N8, N30, N31, N37 to Tron)   Rail: Waverley (close)

11 - 11(1am Fri, 2am Sat); Closed Sun

Caledonian Deuchars IPA[H] ☺

Unusual shaped long pub up an Old Town close. A carpeted lounge-type area, decorated with a long-case clock and historical photos, ends in a large stained glass window. Occasional Geordieoke.

OD (terrasse de fumeur)   BS

Jolly Judge

G5

7a James Court, EH1 2PB

(0131) 225 2669

Bus: Lothian 23, 27, 41, 42, 45, N27   Rail: Waverley

12(12.30 Sun) - 11(Midnight Fri & Sat)

Beer Range (2) Varies[H] ☺

Cosy bar, hidden down Old Town close just off the Royal Mile. Handy for those in need of liquid sustenance after a hard day touring Edinburgh Castle. Beers are often from Scottish micros. In summer literary tours start from here. Occasional university philosophy tutorials are also seen, and heard. A Rebus tryst pub - which novel?

OD (pavement tables)   ML (12-2)   BS   DW (after 2pm)

Kay's Bar

S4

39 Jamaica Street, EH3 6HF (off India St.)

(0131) 225 1858

Bus: Lothian 24, 29, 42

11 - Midnight(1am Fri & Sat); 12.30 - 11 Sun

Caledonian Deuchars IPA; Theakston's Best Bitter; 5 Guest Beers[H] ☺

Small, cosy and convivial pub haunted by lawyers in the early evening. There is an impressive range of beers for the size of the bar. One wall is decorated with whisky barrels, and there is also a good whisky selection behind the bar. The even smaller back room holds a well stocked library. The lunches consist of mainly traditional Scottish fare. The building was once used as a wine merchant and the remains of the pipes can still be seen around the light rose.

ML (12-2.30)   BS   DW (after 2.30pm)

Kenilworth D3

152 Rose Street, EH2 3JD

(0131) 226 1773

Bus: City Centre   Rail: Waverley

11(12.30 Sun) - 11(Midnight Fri & Sat)   ☺

Caledonian Deuchars IPA, 80; 3 Guest Beers[H]

Classic Edinburgh pub with ornate high ceiling and island bar with carved wooden gantry. Listed on CAMRA'S national pub inventory. The walls are tiled and there is a massive old Drybrough mirror. Small lounge to rear is a family room during the day.

DA   OD (pavement tables)   MD (12-9)   BS   CW

Kings Wark V2

36 The Shore, EH6 6QU

(0131) 554 9260

Bus: Lothian 16, 22, 35, 36, N22

12(10 Fri; 11 Sun) - 10.45(11.30 Fri; 11.45 Sat)

Caledonian Deuchars IPA, 80; Guest Beer[H]   ☺

On the ground floor of a tenement building, near Water of Leith. Divided into several areas with wooden furniture. Nominated for "Best Pub Grub" in Scottish restaurant award 2008.

ML (12(11 Sun)-3)   ME (6-10)   BS   CW (during day)

Last Drop Tavern F6

74 Grassmarket, EH1 2JR

(0131) 225 4851

Bus: Lothian 2 (or 23, 27, 41, 42, 45, N27 to George IV Bridge)   Rail: Waverley

11(12.30 Sun) - 1

Caledonian Deuchars IPA[P]   ☺

Elderly bar with many makeovers, such as supplementing the real beams with ersatz beams. Fine collection of paper money above the serving area.

OD (pavement tables)   MD (12-9)   BS   CW   DW

Lauriston Farm O3

69 Lauriston Farm Rd., EH4 5EX

(0131) 312 7071

Bus: Lothian 16, 27, 29, 37, 42, N8, N37

11(12 Sun) - 11

Caledonian Deuchars IPA or 80[H]

Brewer's Fayre establishment in a large stone built farm building with a strong bias towards families and food.

DA   OD (garden with play area)   MD (11.30(12 Sun)-10)   BS   CW

Leslies Bar U7

45 Ratcliffe Terrace, EH9 1SU

(0131) 667 7205

Bus: Lothian 42

11 - 11(11.30 Thu; 12.30am Fri & Sat); 12.30 - 11.30 Sun

Caledonian Deuchars IPA, 80; Taylor Landlord; 2 Guest Beers[H]   ☺

Outstanding Victorian pub, listed on CAMRA's pub inventory. It retains its fine ceiling, cornice, leaded glass work and half wood panelling. The island bar has a spectacular snob screen which divides the pub. Small `ticket window` hatches allow customers to order drinks. A plaque near the fire place gives further details of this busy, vibrant but orderly pub. The 3 guest beers are usually from smaller breweries. Regular live Jazz on Mon eve.

BS   DW

Links Hotel S6

2-4 Alvanley Terrace, EH9 1DU

(0131) 229 3834

Bus: Lothian 11, 15/15A, 16, 17, 23, 45, N11, N16

9(12.30 Sun) - 1am

Caledonian Deuchars IPA, 80[P]   ☺

A sports bar within a hotel. Overlooks the attractive Bruntsfield Links, with an extensive patio drinking area. Handy for a pint after a game at the nearby historic 36 hole pitch & put.

AC   DA   OD (patio)   MD   BS   CW (if eating)

Lloyds No 1 T4

Omni Leisure Centre

(0131) 524 7760

Bus: Lothian 1, 4, 5, 7, 8, 10, 11, 12, 14, 15/15A, 16, 17, 19, 22, 25, 26, 34, 44/44A, 45, 49, N3, N8, N11, N16, N22, N25, N26, N37, N44   Rail: Waverley

10(12.30 Sun) - 1am

Caledonian Deuchars IPA, 80; GK Abbot Ale;
Weston's Old Rosie Cider[H] ☺

Airy, modern, open plan bar in modern entertainment complex, adjacent to the Playhouse Theatre. Part of the J D Wetherspoon's chain. Music can be loud in the evenings.

DA   OD (patio at front)   MD (9-11)   BS   CW (until 8pm)

Malt and Hops   V2

45 The Shore, EH6 6QU

(0131) 555 0083

Bus: Lothian 16, 22, 35, 36, N22

12(12.30 Sun) - 11(Midnight Wed & Thu; 1am Fri & Sat)

Caledonian Deuchars IPA; Marston Pedigree Bitter; 6 Guest Beers[H] ☺

One roomed public bar dating from 1749 and in the heart of `new` Leith's riverside restaurant district. Wood panelling gives an intimate feel with numerous mirrors, artefacts and a large oil painting adding interest. The superb collection of pump clips, many from now defunct breweries, indicate the ever-changing interesting range of guest beers, often from Scottish breweries.

OD (pavement tables)   ML (not Sat & Sun)   BS   CW (until 6pm)   DW

Malt Shovel Inn   H4

11-15 Cockburn Street, EH1 1BP

(0131) 225 6843

Bus: Lothian 36, Airlink 100, (or City Centre) Rail: Waverley (close)

12(12.30 Mon & Wed & Sun) - 11(Midnight Tue & Thu; 1am Fri & Sat)   ☺

Caledonian Deuchars IPA, 80; 2 Guest Beers[H]

Busy, city centre pub divided into 3 areas of differing character. The bar, with attractive wooden gantry, is Robert Adam baroque with mirrored sides. Good selection of malt whisky. Live Jazz on Tue eve. Scottish music on Thu eve.

OD (pavement tables)   MD (12-6)   BS

Maltings Ale House   U6

81 St. Leonards Street, EH8 9QY

(0131) 667 5946

Bus: Lothian 2

12(12.30 Sun) - 1am

Beer range (3) Varies[H]

Wooden floored alehouse with wood panelled walls and wooden furniture. Popular with students and features a video jukebox and pool table.

DA   OD (pavement tables)   DW

McCowan's Brewhouse   R6

Fountain Park Complex, EH11 1AF

(0131) 228 8198

Bus: Lothian 1, 22, 30, 34, 35, N22, N30   Rail: Haymarket

12(12.30 Sun) - 1am(Midnight Mon)

Caledonian Deuchars IPA; John Smith's Cask Bitter; 4 Guest Beers[H] ☺

American style brew pub, with on-site brewery (not used June 08). Split onto 2 levels with a glass front wall giving a light and airy feel. Furnished with a mixture of tables and chairs and comfy armchairs, but exposed metal roof beams and ducts give an industrial ambiance.

DA   OD (terrace)   MD (until 9)   BS   CW (until 6pm)

Meadow Bar   U6

42-44 Buccleuch St., EH8 9PL

(0131) 667 6907

Bus: Lothian 41, 42

11(12 Sun) - 1am

Caledonian Deuchars IPA, 80[H]

Walk-in, well appointed lounge bar on the ground floor of a tenement.

MD (12-8(5 Sat); Not Sun)   CW (until 8pm)   DW

Melville Lounge   S5

25 William Street, EH3 7NG

(0131) 225 1011

Bus: Lothian 3/3A, 4, 12, 25, 26, 31, 33, 44/44A, X48, N3, N25, N26, N31, N44   Rail: Haymarket

11(12.30 Sun) - Midnight(1am Thu-Sat)

Caledonian Deuchars IPA, 80[H]

Nicely decorated, comfortable lounge bar with seating throughout. Can be busy, but no apparent loud music.

OD (at front)   ML (12-3)   ME (6-10)   BS   CW (until 8pm)

Menzies Belford Hotel   R5

69 Belford Road, EH4 3DW

(0131) 332 2545

Bus: Lothian 13

10.30(11.30 Sun) - Midnight(1am Fri & Sat)

Caledonian Deuchars IPA[P]

The Granary is a comfortable modern bar in a converted mill, built in 1807, at the rear of the hotel. The Water of Leith runs beside the beer garden.

AC DA OD (courtyard & garden) MD (12-9.30) BS CW DW

Mercat   R5

28 West Maitland Street, EH12 5DX

(0131) 225 8716

Bus: Lothian 3/3A, 4, 12, 25, 26, 31, 33, 44/44A, N3, N25, N26, N31, N44 Rail: Haymarket (close)

9am(12.30 Sun) - 1am

Caledonian Deuchars IPA; Occasional Guest Beer[H]

Refurbished bar just off Haymarket. An additional basement bar (no real ale) opens when busy. Comedy on Mon. evenings. Poetry on first Thu. of the month.

OD (balcony) MD (9(12.30 Sun)-9) BS

Milnes   F2

35 Hanover St, EH2 2PJ

(0131) 225 6738

Bus: City Centre Rail: Waverley

10(12.30 Sun) - 11(Midnight Thu; 1am Fri & Sat)

Caledonian Deuchars IPA, 80; 3 Guest Beers[H]

Historic pub which has recently been refurbished. Can be busy at weekends but has a number of rooms on several levels with plenty of seating.

DA (upstairs bar) OD (pavement tables) MD (10-10) BS CW (if over 14)

Minders   U7

114 Causewayside, EH9 1PU

(0131) 667 9479

Bus: Lothian 42

11(12.30 Sun) - 11(Midnight Fri & Sat)

Caledonian Deuchars IPA; Guest Beer (summer)[H]

Comfortable modern suburban lounge bar in an old building. The original cornices are retained.

DW

Mitre   J4

131 High Street, EH1 1SG

(0131) 652 3902

Bus: Lothian 3/3A, 5, 7, 8, 14, 29, 30, 31, 33, 35, 37, 47, X47, X48, 49, N3, N8, N30, N31, N37 Rail: Waverley

10 - Midnight(1am Fri & Sat)

Caledonian Deuchars IPA; Marston's Pedigree[H] ☺

Lively bar popular with tourists and locals. Olde world style, with bookshelves and pictures of old Edinburgh. Large eating area to the rear.

OD (pavement tables) MD BS CW (until 8pm)

Montpeliers   S7

159-161 Bruntsfield Place, EH10 4DG

(0131) 229 3115

Bus: Lothian 11, 15/15A, 16, 17, 23, 45, N11, N16

11(12.30 Sun) - 1am

Caledonian Deuchars IPA, 80[P]

Trendy bistro bar which provides a quiet haven during the day. In the evening it can become very busy and you may struggle to find a table.

OD (pavement tables) MD (breakfasts from 9am) BS CW (until 8pm, if eating)

Morningside Glory   S7

1-5 Comiston Road, EH10 6AA

(0131) 447 1205

Bus: Lothian 5, 11, 15/15A, 16, 23, 38, 41 Craighouse, N11, N16

10 - Midnight(1am Thu-Sat)

Caledonian Deuchars IPA, 80; Guest Beer (Ocasional) [H]

Situated at the apex of a busy road junction, this pub has a high corniced ceiling and an extensive semi-circular windowed frontage. Stone-clad pillars dominate the floor and a steel bar top gives a modern feel.

DA OD (pavement seats) MD (12(10 Thu-Sat)-9) BS CW (until 8pm) DW

Mortonhall Golf Club   S10

231 Braid Road, EH10 6BP

(0131) 447 2411

Bus: Lothian 11, 15/15A, N11

Stewart Pentland IPA

Members only golf club

Nobles   V2

44a Constitution Street, EH6 6RS

(0131) 554 2024

Bus: Lothian 16, 35

Caledonian Deuchars IPA, 80/-[H] ☺

Large pub with Victorian interior and interesting facade. WARNING: Closed April 08 following fire damage.

Old Bell   U7

233 Causewayside, EH9 1PH

(0131) 668 1573

Bus: Lothian 5, 42

11(12.30 Sun) - 11.45(12.45am Fri & Sat)

Caledonian Deuchars IPA, Guest Beer[H] ☺

Comfortable pub with olde world appearance due to wooden carved panels and cornice, including fishing and golf sections. The decor includes numerous bells. Large TV screens show sport.

OD (pavement tables)   ML (12(12.30 Sun)-2.30(3 weekends))   ME (5.30-7)   BS   CW (if eating)   DW (not food times)

Old Chain Pier   S1

32 Trinity Crescent, EH5 3ED

(0131) 552 1233

Bus: Lothian 16 (or 7, 11, N11 Newhaven)

11(12.30 Sun) - 11(Midnight Thu-Sat)

Caledonian Deuchars IPA; Greene King Abbot Ale; Taylor's Landlord; Guest Beer[H] ☺

The place to go for superb sea views. This cosy pub has a wooden interior with a nautical theme. The new conservatory is perfect for family meals. 10% reduction on the imaginative food for card carrying CAMRA members.

OD (pavement tables)   MD (12-8.30(9.30 Summer))   BS   CW (until 7pm, in conservatory)

Old Dock Bar   U2

3-5 Dock Place, EH6 6LV

(0131) 553 7223

Bus: Lothian 16, 22, 35, 36, N22

12(12.30 Sun) - 11(1am Fri & Sat)

3 Guest Beers[H] ☺

Small traditional bar adjoining a large restaurant. The walls are decorated with maritime prints and photographs of old Leith. Now home of the original 8 handpump bank from Todd's Tap. The building has been a bar since 1813, and claims to be Leith's oldest. Convenient for visitors to the Scottish Government offices and Ocean Terminal shopping centre. Good quality meals served.

DA   OD (seats at rear)   MD   BS   CW

Olde Inn   O3

25 Main Street, EH4 5BZ

(0131) 336 2437

Bus: Lothian 21, 24, 41

11(12.30 Sun) - 11(Midnight Fri & Sat)

Caledonian Deuchars IPA, 80, Guest Beer[H]

Village local which appeals to all age groups. The comfortable lounge, with dark wooden furniture and tapestry seats, is decorated with horse brasses. To the rear is a large conservatory area. The public bar is host to darts and golf teams, and has several TVs for sport.

OD (garden with play area)   MD (12(12.30 Sun)-8)   BS   CW (until 8pm, not bar)   DW (bar only)

Orchard   T4

1 Howard Place, EH3 5JZ

(0131) 550 0850

Bus: Lothian 8, 17, 23, 27, N8

11 - Midnight(1am Fri & Sat); 12.30 - 11 Sun

Black Sheep Bitter; Caledonian Deuchars IPA[H] ☺

Much altered open plan pub with varied seating areas and some surviving stained glass in the windows. Upmarket, restaurant style food (tables can be reserved). Flat screens show major sporting events. Occasional live music and quizzes.

OD (pavement tables)   MD (12-8.30)   BS   CW (until 8pm)

Ormelie Bar   Z5

44 Joppa Road, EH15 2ET

(0131) 669 3323

Bus: Lothian 15/15A, 26, N26

11 - Midnight(12.45am Fri & Sat); 12.30 - 11 Sun

Caledonian Deuchars IPA; Stewart 80/-; 2 Guest Beers[H] ☺

A historic tenement lounge bar, converted from a shop in late 19c, and situated close to Portobello promenade. This welcoming locals' pub features a lovely long bar surrounded by ornate lanterns. The gantry is stocked with a huge array of malt whiskies. Historic photos and golf memorabilia adorn the walls.

BS DW

Oxford Bar   C2

8 Young Street, EH2 4JB

(0131) 539 7119

Bus: City Centre

11 - Midnight(1am Thu-Sat); 12.30 - 11 Sun

Caledonian Deuchars IPA; 2 Guest Beers[H] ☺

Small, basic, vibrant, New Town, drinking shop decorated with Scottishesque memorabilia. It is one of the favourite pubs of Rebus and his creator. It has been the haunt of many other famous and infamous characters over the years so you never know who you might bump into. Why not visit the website and contribute a story. A real taste of New Town past and listed on CAMRA's national pub inventory.

BS DW

Pavilion   S10

47 Buckstone Terrace, EH10 6QJ

(0131) 445 5584

Bus: Lothian 11, 15/15A, N11

11(12.30 Sun) - Midnight

Caledonian Deuchars IPA; Guest Beer[H]

Purpose built, comfortable, suburban lounge bar within easy striking distance of Robert Louis Stevenson's childhood home of Swanston. The adjoining restaurant, Tusitala, is open for meals until 9pm.

DA OD (deck at front) MD (until 8) BS CW (until 8pm) DW

Peacock Inn   S2

Newhaven Road, EH6 4HZ

(0131) 552 5522

Bus: Lothian 7, 10, 11, 16, N11

11(12.30 Sun) - 11

Guest Beer[H] ☺

Established in 1767 in Newhaven fishing village. Famous for haddock (try the "whale") with dedicated restaurant. A photo gallery has pictures of bygone days.

OD (patio at front) MD (until 9.45) CW

Pearce's   U4

23 Elm Row, EH7 4AA

(0131) 556 4140

Bus: Lothian 7, 10, 11, 12, 14, 16, 22, 25, 49, N11, N22, N25

11(12.30 Sun) - Midnight(1am Fri & Sat)

Caledonian Deuchars IPA[H] ☺

Recently refurbished food orientated pub, with an eclectic mix of furniture, on two levels. The upper level holds ever changing art exhibitions. Music played throughout, but no TVs.

OD (pavement tables) MD (11-10) BS CW

Peartree House   J8

38 West Nicolson Street, EH8 9DD

(0131) 667 7533

Bus: Lothian 41, 42 (or 2, 3/3A, 5, 7, 8, 14, 29, 30, 31, 33, 37, 47, X47, X48, 49, N3, N8, N30, N31, N37 to Nicholson St) Rail: Waverley

11(12.30 Sun) - Midnight(1am Fri & Sat)

Caledonian Deuchars IPA[P]

A single large room, in an 18th century building, with a square island bar, comfy leather sofas, a real fire, two TVs and a big screen. Very popular beer garden, with summer barbecues. The Deuchars is real, despite the appearance of the fount.

OD (paved walled garden) BS

The Regent

CAMRA 2008 Edinburgh and overall Edinburgh & SE Scotland Pub of the Year

Phoenix
T4

46-48a Broughton Street, EH1 3SA

(0131) 557 0234

Bus: Lothian 8, 17, N8 (or 4, 10, 11, 12, 15/15A, 16, 26, 44/44A, 45 to York Place)   Rail: Waverley

10(12.30 Sun) - 1am

Caledonian Deuchars IPA, 80[P]

Recently altered from its esoteric 70s atmosphere into a cafe bar style. A large bar area, with a separate raised section. It's hard to tell there's real ale as it's mixed in with the banks of keg beer taps.

BS

Queens Arms
D2

49 Frederick Street, EH2 1EP

(0131) 225 1045

Bus: City Centre   Rail: Waverley

10(12 Sun) - 1am

Caledonian Deuchars IPA, 80; Guest Beer[H] ☺

Large basement pub dominated by an island bar with some cubicle style seating. Named after Mary Queen of Scots.

OD (pavement tables)   MD   BS

Regent
V4

2 Montrose Terrace, EH7 5DL

(0131) 661 8198

Bus: Lothian 35 (or 1, 4, 5, 15/15A, 19, 26, 34, 44/44A, 45, N26, N44 to London Rd)

11(12.30 Sun) - 1am

Caledonian Deuchars IPA; 3 Guest Beers[H] ☺

Large, tenement bar with two rooms, one being music free. The comfortable seating consists of banquettes, leather sofas and armchairs. Popular with gay and lesbian real ale drinkers and offering an interesting range of three guest beers. A novel slant on pub games is the gymnastic pommel horse by the toilets. CAMRA Edinburgh pub of the year 2008, and overall winner for SE Scotland. Free Wi-Fi access available.

MD BS DW

Reverie U6

1-5 Newington Road, EH9 1QR

(0131) 667 8870

Bus: Lothian 3/3A, 5, 7, 8, 14, 29, 30, 31, 33, 37, 47, 49, N3, N8, N30, N31, N37

11(12.30 Sun) - 11

Caledonian Deuchars IPA[H]

L-shaped lounge bar with claret coloured interior.

ML ME BS

Robbies Bar U3

367 Leith Walk, EH6 8SE

(0131) 554 6850

Bus: Lothian 7, 10, 11, 12, 13, 14, 16, 22, 25, 49, N11, N22, N25

12(11 Sat; 12.30 Sun) - Midnight

Caledonian Deuchars IPA, 80; Guest Beer[H] ☺

Traditional small locals' pub. Interesting mirrors on wall. Busy early evening and very popular with sports enthusiasts. Live music some weekends.

DA OD (pavement tables)

Rose & Crown C3

170 Rose Street, EH2 4BA

(0131) 226 5646

Bus: City Centre   Rail: Waverley

11 - 1am

Caledonian Deuchars IPA; Guest Beer[H] ☺

Recently refurbished L shaped lounge bar with a raised seating area to rear.

OD (pavement tables)   MD (12-6)   BS

Rose St. Brewery E3

55 Rose Street, EH2 2NH

(0131) 220 1227

Bus: City Centre   Rail: Waverley

12(12.30 Sun) - 11(1am Fri & Sat)

Caledonian Deuchars IPA, 80; Occasional Guest Beer[H] ☺

2 levelled bar, part carpeted and part with flagstone floor. Various historical artefacts around the bar. No longer contains a brewery.

OD (pavement tables)   MD (12-9)   BS

Roseburn Bar R5

1 Roseburn Terrace, EH12 5NG

(0131) 337 1067

Bus: Lothian 12, 26, 31, N26, N31   Rail: Haymarket

11(12.30 Sun) - 11(Midnight Thu-Sat)

Caledonian Deuchars IPA[P]

Traditional pub with high ceilings and interesting mirrors in the public bar. A small, comfortable lounge bar has period photos. Handy for Murrayfield. WARNING: Caledonian 80/- maybe advertised on a traditional fount but only the keg version is available.

DA   OD (pavement tables)   BS   DW

Roseleaf U2

23-24 Sandport Place, EH6 6EW

(0131) 467 9864

Bus: Lothian 16, 22, 35, 36, N22

10 - Midnight(1am Fri & Sat)

Caledonian Deuchars IPA; Guest Beer[H] ☺

Once the "Black Swan", the birthplace of Edinburgh CAMRA. The bar has the original wood panelling and furnished with an eclectic collection of tables and chairs. There is also a back room.

OD (pavement bench)   MD (10-10)   BS   CW

Royal Ettrick Hotel R7

13 Ettrick Road, EH10 5BJ

(0131) 228 6413

Bus: Lothian 10, 27, N27

9am - Midnight(1am Fri & Sat)

Caledonian Deuchars IPA[H]

Dating from 1875, this hotel in a large suburban villa has a well appointed lounge bar and conservatory extensions. TV screens near the bar show todays live sport.

AC   OD (garden)   MD   CW   DW

Royal McGregor I4

154 High Street, EH1 1QS

(0131) 225 7064

Bus: Lothian 3/3A, 5, 7, 8, 14, 29, 30, 31, 33, 35, 37, 47, X47, X48, 49, N3, N8, N30, N31, N37
Rail: Waverley

9.30(12.30 Sun) - Midnight(1am Fri & Sat)

Caledonian Deuchars IPA, 2 Guest Beers[H]

Long rectangular seating area with, in the main, plain tables. The bar features a nice gantry. The clientele is mainly tourists and it can get quite busy.

OD (pavement tables) MD (9.30-11) CW (until 8pm, if over 14)

Royal Oak   J6

1 Infirmary Street, EH1 1LT

(0131) 557 2976

Bus: Lothian 3/3A, 5, 7, 8, 14, 29, 30, 31, 33, 35, 37, 47, X47, 49, N3, N8, N30, N31, N37   Rail: Waverley

10(12.30 Sun) - 2am

Caledonian Deuchars IPA; Guest Beer[P] ☺

Small plain bar just off South Bridge. Impromptu folk music evenings are a regular occurrence, whilst the downstairs bar hosts more formal events. Rebus tours leave from here during summer. Good selection of single malt whiskies at competitive prices.

BS DW

Rumba   U2

17 Portland Place, EH6 6LA

(0131) 467 7227

Bus: Lothian 16, 22, 35, 36, N22

3 - 1am

Stewart Pentland IPA

Primarily a rum and rum based cocktail bar, Rumba is small and cosy with comfortable seating and a laid back atmosphere. Open mic nights weekly.

BS DW

Ryan's Bar   B4

2 Hope Street, EH2 4DB

(0131) 226 6669

Bus: City Centre Rail: Haymarket

10 - Midnight(1am Fri & Sat)

Caledonian Deuchars IPA[P]

Popular cafe bar in prominent West End location. An old building with glass extensions giving a modern appearance. Coffee shop and outdoor tables offer splendid views of the city.

DA OD (pavement tables) MD (9am-10) BS CW (not main bar) DW

Ryries   R5

1 Haymarket Terrace, EH12 5EY

(0131) 337 7582

Bus: Lothian 2, 3/3A, 4, 12, 25, 26, 31, 33, 44/44A, X48, N3, N25, N26, N31, N44   Rail: Haymarket (close)

9am(12.30 Sun) - 1am

Caledonian Deuchars IPA, 80[H] ☺

Classic Scottish bar, on two levels, with dark wooden interior, fine bar gantry and stained glass windows. Attracts a varied clientele, with TV sport being very popular. An upstairs function room has been converted into a Bistro.

MD (12-7) BS CW (new bistro only)

Sandy Bells   H7

25 Forrest Road, EH1 2QH

(0131) 225 2751

*Bus: Lothian 2, 23, 27, 35, 41, 42, 45, N27
Rail: Waverley*

11.30 - 1am; 12.30 - 11 Sun

Caledonian Deuchars IPA, 80; Courage Director's; Inveralmond Ossian's Ale[H] ☺

This pub, featuring an arch and dark wood panelling, has been part of the Edinburgh traditional music scene for many years. Folk music is played every night. A must visit for all, not just music lovers.

DW (bowl & biscuits provided)

Scotsman Lounge   I4

73 Cockburn St., EH1 1BU

(0131) 225 7726

*Bus: Lothian 3/3A, 5, 7, 8, 14, 29, 30, 31, 33, 35, 37, 47, X47, X48, 49, N3, N8, N30, N31, N37
Rail: Waverley*

6am(12.30 Sun) - 1am

Caledonian Deuchars IPA

Single roomed bar with live music every evening. Can be very busy and noisy. Photographs of piped bands adorn the walls.

Scott's Bar   C3

202 Rose Street, EH2 4AZ

(0131) 225 7401

Bus: City Centre   Rail: Waverley

11(12.30 Sun) - 1am

Caledonian Deuchars IPA, 80[H]

Wooden floored alehouse at the start or end of the Rose St. crawl. The single L shaped room is dominated by a circular bar counter. WARNING: Closed June 08. Check details before visit.

OD (pavement tables)

Scruffy Murphy's   S5

13 Melville Place., EH3 7PR

(0131) 226 3404

Bus: Lothian 13, 19, 36, 37, 41, 47, X47, N37 Rail: Haymarket

10(12 Sun) - Midnight(1.30am Fri & Sat)

Caledonian Deuchars IPA[H]

Irish style basement bar with wooden interior and friendly atmosphere. Can be noisy with live bands on Friday and Saturday evenings.

MD (12-6)   BS

Shakespeare   B6

65 Lothian Road, EH1 2DJ

(0131) 228 8400

Bus: Lothian 1, 10, 11, 15/15A, 16, 17, 22, 24, 30, 34, N11, N16, N22, N30   Rail: Haymarket

11(12.30 Sun) - Midnight(1am Fri & Sat)

Caledonian Deuchars IPA; guest Beer[H] ☺

Comfortable, spacious lounge-like bar whose seating comprises sofas, chairs and banquettes. Mon quiz, Sat karaoke. 5 plasma screens for sports. Extremely handy for the Usher Hall, Filmhouse, Traverse and Lyceum.

OD (pavement tables)   MD (12-9)   BS

Sheep Heid Inn   W6

43 The Causeway, EH15 3QA

(0131) 656 6951

Bus: Lothian 42

11(12 Sun) - 11(Midnight Fri & Sat)

Beer Range (3) Varies[A] ☺

Historic pub, dating from the 14th century, with several drinking areas. The comfortable lounge has dark wood panelling. A skittle alley at the rear can be hired.

DA   OD (courtyard)   ML   ME   CW (until 8pm) DW (bar & courtyard)

Shore   V2

3 Shore, EH6 6QW

(0131) 553 5080

Bus: Lothian 16, 22, 35, 36, N22

12(12.30 Sun) - 1am(12.30am Sun)

Caledonian Deuchars IPA; Guest Beer[P] ☺

Popular riverfront bar and restaurant with wooden interior. The high ceiling and large mirror lend space to the otherwise small bar. The separate restaurant offers seafood specialities. Live music Tues and Wed evenings.

OD (pavement tables)   MD (12-10.30)   CW   DW

Smithies Ale House   T4

49-51 Eyre Place, EH3 5EY

(0131) 556 9805

Bus: Lothian 8, 13, 17, 36, N8 (or 23, 27 to Canonmills)

11(12.30 Sun) - Midnight(12.30am Fri-Sun)

Caledonian Deuchars IPA; Guest Beer[H]

Small, friendly pub featuring hand-painted mirrors of flora and fauna along with a horseshoe bar. Nice place for a quiet drink although often has music and/or sport on the TV. Win a gallon of beer in the Thursday quiz.

OD (pavement tables)   ML (12-2.30 Mon-Fri)   BS

Southsider   K8

3/5 West Richmond Street, EH8 9EF

(0131) 667 2003

Bus: Lothian 2, 3/3A, 5, 7, 8, 14, 29, 30, 31, 33, 37, 47, X47, X48, 49, N3, N8, N30, N31, N37 Rail: Waverley

11(12.30 Sun) - Midnight(1am Fri & Sat)

Caledonian Deuchars IPA; 2 Guest Beers[H] ☺

Lounge bar, with large sofas, popular with locals and students. Two TVs and big screen. The public bar has seating booths and a pool table. Live music on Sat and a quiz on Wed evenings.

MD (11-7)   BS

Spylaw Tavern   O10

27 Spylaw Street, EH13 OJT

(0131) 441 2783

Bus: Lothian 10, 16 Colinton, 18, 45, N16

11 - Midnight; 12 - 11 Sun

Caledonian Deuchars IPA; 2 Guest Beers [H] ☺

Attractive pub with bar, lounge, restaurant and secure beer garden set in historic Colinton village. The decor gives the bar a light airy feel due to the use of light coloured wood. The lounge is well appointed and the restaurant has views over the Dell. All food is freshly prepared on the premises including a range of pies that are a speciality. The pub makes an ideal stop when walking the Water of Leith path.

DA   OD (beer garden)   MD (until 9(7.30 Sun))   BS CW (if eating)

St. Vincent Bar   S4

11 St. Vincent Street, EH3 6SJ

(0131) 225 7447

Bus: Lothian 24, 29, 42

11(12.30 Sun) - Midnight(1am Fri & Sat)

Caledonian Deuchars IPA; 4 Guest Beers[H] ☺

Unpretentious but comfortable New Town basement pub with beautiful stained glass windows. The bar has a fine gantry incorporating a clock. Brass cribbage boards are built into some of the tables. Also a pool table.

OD (patio tables)   ML (12-3)   ME (5-8)   BS   CW (lunchtime only)   DW

Stable Bar   U11

Mortonhall Park, EH16 6TJ

(0131) 664 0773

Bus: Lothian 11 Hyvots Bank, 18, N11

11(12.30 Sun) - 11(Midnight summer)

Caledonian Deuchars IPA; Stewart Pentland IPA, Copper Cascade[H] ☺

A real country pub on the edge of the city. Numerous paths are ideal for exploring the surrounding woods. The comfortable bar is dominated by the large stone fireplace, which boasts a roaring log fire in the winter. A plainer back room is mainly for diners. With the real ales coming from breweries less than three miles away, this is a true local pub. Watch out for the Little Miss Muffet seat.

OD (courtyard)   MD (12-9(10 summer))   CW   DW

Standard   S4

24 Howe St, EH3 6TG

(0131) 225 6490

Bus: Lothian 24, 29, 42

11(12.30 Sun) - Midnight(1am Fri & Sat)

Caledonian Deuchars IPA[P]

Long, thin New Town bar with interesting gallery of photographs and architectural touches and fittings.

OD (pavement tables)   MD (11-9)   BS

Standing Order   E2

62-66 George St., EH2 2LR

(0131) 225 4460

Bus: City Centre   Rail: Waverley

9(12.30 Sun) - 1am

Caledonian Deuchars IPA, 80; Many Guest Beers[H] ☺

Built in 1879 to a Robert Adam design, the once head office of the British Linen Bank was converted into a vast pub in 1997 by JD Wetherspoon. The main bar has a superb high ceiling and polished granite pillars. Smaller rooms lead off, one containing the old Chubb vault door. Despite its size it can be very busy at times, however it lacks atmosphere when quiet.

DA (stair lift at Rose St. entrance)   OD (pavement tables)   MD   BS   CW (until 8pm)

Star Bar   T4

1 Northumberland Place, EH3 6LQ

(0131) 539 8070

Bus: Lothian 13, 23, 27   Rail: Waverley

12 - 1am

Caledonian Deuchars IPA[H] ☺

Tucked away in a New Town side street, this locals bar has an L shaped split level layout. The upper level has a food serving area, while the lower level has the bar and a table football machine.

OD (garden)   ML (12-3)   ME (weekends only)   BS CW (garden only)   DW

Starbank Inn   T1

64 Laverockbank Road, EH5 3BZ

(0131) 552 4141

Bus: Lothian 16 (or 7, 11, N11 to Newhaven)

11(12.30 Sun) - 11(Midnight Thu-Sat)

Belhaven Sandy Hunters Ale, 80/-; Caledonian Deuchars IPA; Taylor Landlord; 4 Guest Beers [H] ☺

Bright, airy, bare-boarded ale house, with a U-shaped layout extending into a conservatory dining area. The walls sport several rare brewery mirrors. Enjoy the superb views across the Firth to Fife. At least four interesting guest ales, often from Scottish independent breweries, are usually available. Occasional jazz on Sundays.

DA   OD (patio`)   ML   ME   MD (Sat & Sun)   BS   CW (until 8.30pm)   DW (on a lead)

Station Tavern   Q6

316 Gorgie Road, EH11 2QZ

(0131) 337 1062

Bus: Lothian 1, 2, 3/3A, 25, 33, 38, N25

12(12.30 Sun) - 11(Midnight Fri & Sat)

Caledonian Deuchars IPA[H]

Two roomed locals' bar, with pool table, convenient for Tynecastle and Murrayfield.

DA   OD (pavement tables)

Struan Hotel   O6

3-4 Downie Terrace, EH12 7AU

(0131) 539 7064

Bus: Lothian 12, 26, 31, N26, N31

11(12 Sun) - Midnight(1am Fri & Sat)

Caledonian Deuchars IPA[H]

Quiet, comfortable, lounge bar in hotel with listed frontage, opposite Edinburgh Zoo and close to Murrayfield stadium. Can get busy at lunchtimes. Also a small bar area and restaurant /function rooms.

AC   OD (garden)   ML (12-2)   ME (6-9)   BS   CW

Tass   K4

1 Jeffrey Street, EH1 1SR

(0131) 556 6338

Bus: Lothian 35, 36   Rail: Waverley

11(12.30 Sun) - Midnight(1am Fri & Sat)

Caledonian Deuchars IPA; 3 Guest Beers[H] ☺

Wooden floored bar serving a mixture of real ales, malt whiskies and fine wines to locals, tourists and musicians. A small eating room leads off. Live traditional music sessions Mon and Wed-Fri. Beer available in 1/3 pint glasses.

MD (12-9)   BS   CW (until 9pm, if eating)

Teuchters   S5

26 William Street

(0131) 225 2973

Bus: Lothian 3/3A, 4, 12, 25, 26, 31, 33, 44/44A, X48, N3, N25, N26, N31, N44   Rail: Haymarket

11(12.30 Sun) - 1am

Caledonian Deuchars IPA; Harviestoun Schiehallion; Orkney Dark Island; Taylor Landlord[H] ☺

A comfortable half wood panelled bar with a nice mural where you can sit and read the newspaper. Food is only available in the downstairs restaurant.

ML (12-2.30)   ME (5.30-10)   BS

Teuchter's Landing   U2

1c Dock Place, EH6 6LU

(0131) 554 7427

Bus: Lothian 16, 22, 35, 36, N22

12 - 11(Midnight Fri & Sat)

Caledonian Deuchars IPA; Inveralmond Ossian; Taylor Landlord[H] ☺

Formally the Waterfront Wine Bar. To the front is a small bar where the wall is half wood panelled, half stone with the names of the old east coast ferry drop off points listed around the top. The ceiling is also wood panelled. To the rear is a larger restaurant and bistro, with a conservatory extension that opens out onto a pontoon floating on the Water of Leith. New owners in March 2008.

DA   OD   MD   CW (in conservatory)

Theatre Royal   U4

25-27 Greenside Place, EH1 3AA

(0131) 557 2142

Bus: Lothian 1, 4, 5, 7, 8, 10, 11, 12, 14, 15/15A, 16, 17, 19, 22, 25, 26, 34, 44/44A, 45, 49, N3, N8, N11, N16, N22, N25, N26, N37, N44   Rail: Waverley

12(12.30 Sun) - Midnight (1am Fri & Sat)

Caledonian Deuchars IPA; Guest Beer[H] ☺

The heralding pipers in the stonework welcome you to this large, dark wood pub with large island bar. Next door to the Playhouse theatre, so many framed bill posters from shows adorn the walls.

OD (pavement tables)   MD (12-10)   BS   CW (if eating)

Thistle St. Bar E2

39 Thistle Street, EH2 1DY

(0131) 478 7029

Bus: City Centre   Rail: Waverley

12(12.30 Sun) - 1am

Greene King IPA; Guest Beer[P]

Split level bar close to the city centre. Wide selection of interesting whiskies, gins, rums etc. Gourmet pies a speciality. A soup and casserole of the day are available to 9pm.

OD (garden)   MD (until 9)   BS   CW   DW

Thomson's S5

182/4 Morrison Street, EH3 8EB

(0131) 228 5700

Bus: Lothian 2 (or 3/3A, 4, 12, 25, 26, 31, 33, 44/44A, X48, N3, N25, N26, N31, N44 to Haymarket)   Rail: Haymarket

12(4 Sun) - 11.30(Midnight Thu & Sat; 1am Fri)

Caledonian Deuchars IPA; 6 Guest Beers[A] ☺

Modelled on the style of Glasgow architect Alexander 'Greek' Thomson, this award winning pub is dedicated to traditional Scottish air pressure dispense. The superb, custom built gantry features mirrors inlaid with scenes from Greek mythology. The walls are a veritable history of Scottish brewing, with rare mirrors from long defunct Scottish breweries. Guest beers are often from Pictish, Hop Back or Atlas.

OD (pavement tables)   ML (12-2; not Sun; pies only Sat)   BS   DW

Three Monkeys Z5

87 Portobello High St, EH15 1AW

(0131) 669 4533

Bus: Lothian 15/15A, 21 Royal Infirmary, 26, 42, 49, N26

12(12.30 Sun) - Midnight(1am Fri & Sat)

Beer Range (2) Varies[H]

Quiet and friendly pub with a very traditional feel. Lots of wood and leather in evidence. Antiques and artefacts adorn the walls. Small stage for live music on Sat evenings. One of the guest beers is usually from Stewart Brewing.

BS   DW

Tiles Bistro Bar H2

1 St. Andrew Square, EH2 2BD

(0131) 558 1507

Bus: City Centre   Rail: Waverley

11(12 Sun) - 11(Midnight Fri & Sat)

Caledonian Deuchars IPA[P]

Cafe bar in the old Prudential Insurance office. Decorative tiled walls, a high ceiling and huge lamps set the scene. High window seats allow views over St. Andrew Square. Chatting customers and background music create a high-decibel environment.

OD (pavement tables)   MD (not Fri eve)   CW (until 8pm, if eating)

Tolbooth Tavern K4

167 Canongate, EH8 8BN

(0131) 556 5348

Bus: Lothian 35   Rail: Waverley

11(12.30 Sun) - 11(Midnight Fri & Sat)

Caledonian Deuchars IPA, 80[H]

Comfortable split level pub (Est. 1820) in a 16th century building on the historic Royal Mile. Close to Holyrood House, Scottish Parliament, Huntly House & Peoples museums. Views to the rear of Calton Hill.

MD (12-8.30)   BS

Victoria Park Hotel T2

221 Ferry Road, EH6 4NN

(0131) 447 7033

Bus: Lothian 7, 11, 14, 21, N11

11(12.30 Sun) - Midnight

Caledonian Deuchars IPA[H]

The small Gosford Bar is at the rear of the hotel. Recently refurbished, as was the adjacent Otterstone Bar & Grill wherein meals are served. A stone dog guards the garden.

AC   DA   OD (garden & patio)   ME (6-9)   MD (12-9 Sat & Sun)   BS   CW (family room only)

Village Inn U2

16 South Fort Street, EH6 4DN

(0131) 478 7810

Bus: Lothian 7, 14, 21

12(12.30 Sun) - 1am

Caledonian Deuchars IPA[H]

Traditional locals' bar. The bar area is small but the adjoining art gallery/lounge (if not privately booked) provides extra seating. Leith Folk Club meet on Tue. eve. Also a Leith Festival venue.

DW

Villager H5

49-50 George IV Bridge, EH1 1EJ

(0131) 226 2781

Bus: Lothian 23, 27, 35, 41, 42, 45, N27   Rail: Waverley

12 - 1am

Caledonian 80[P]

Trendy and modern bar with limited seating during busy periods, unless dining.

ML (12-5.30) ME (6-9.30) BS

Waiting Room S7

7 Belhaven Terrace, EH10 5HZ

(0131) 452 9707

Bus: Lothian 5, 11, 15/15A, 16, 17, 23, 38, 41 Craighouse, N11, N16

10 - Midnight(1am Fri & Sat)

Caledonian Deuchars IPA; 2 Guest Beers[H]

Large, open plan, modern café-bar on three separate levels with large picture windows. The focus is on food during the day, and it is open for breakfast.

DA   MD (12-9) BS CW (until 9pm, if over 14)

Wally Dug T4

32 Northumberland Street, EH3 6LS

(0131) 556 3271

Bus: Lothian 13, 23, 37 Rail: Waverley

11 - 1am; 12.30 - Midnight Sun

Caledonian Deuchars IPA; Guest Beer[H]   ☺

Cosy New Town basement pub with 2 rooms and an alcove. The back room has lots of old and new books on shelves. Plenty of wally dugs in evidence. Popular with students.

OD (patio tables) BS DW

Waterline V2

10 Burgess Street, EH6 6RD

(0131) 554 2425

Bus: Lothian 16, 22, 35, 36, N22

12(12.30 Sun) - 11(1am Fri & Sat; Midnight Sun)

Greene King IPA; Guest Beer[H]

Split level pub with nautically themed decor and a relaxed atmosphere. The light, airy, front bar looks out onto the Water of Leith. Furnished with a mixture of tables and chairs, sofas and bench seats in booths.

OD (pavement tables) MD (12-9(10 Fri-Sat)) CW (if eating)

Whighams Wine Bar B4

13 Hope Street, EH2 4EL

(0131) 225 8674

Bus: City Centre Rail: Haymarket

12(12.30 Sun) - Midnight(1am Fri & Sat)

Caledonian Deuchars IPA; Guest Beer[H]

Upmarket West End basement bar and restaurant built in General Haig's old wine cellar. Candle lit alcoves lead into a bright and modern dining area. The menu has a Scottish influence with an emphasis on seafood.

OD (terrace) MD BS

Whistle Binkies J5

4-6 South Bridge, EH1 1LL

(0131) 557 5114

Bus: Lothian 3/3A, 5, 7, 8, 14, 29, 30, 31, 33, 35, 37, 47, X47, 49, N3, N8, N30, N31, N37 Rail: Waverley

5(1 Fri-Sun) - 3am

Caledonian Deuchars IPA, 80; Guest Beer[H]   ☺

Plain bar with many alcoves and regular live music. There is an entry fee after midnight on Fri & Sat.

BS DW

White Hart Inn F6

34 Grassmarket, EH1 2JU

(0131) 226 2806

Bus: Lothian 2 (or 23, 27, 41, 42, 45, N27 to George IV Bridge) Rail: Waverley

11(12.30 Sun) - Midnight(1am Fri & Sat)

Caledonian Deuchars IPA, 80; Guest Beer[H]   ☺

Edinburgh's oldest surviving public house with cellarage dating from 1516 and the rest of the building from 1740. A small bar with no TV or fruit machines. Live traditional music Sun 3-6pm. Stag and Hen parties not admitted.

OD (pavement tables)   MD (12-9)   BS   CW (if eating & over 14)

Windsor Buffet   U4

45 Elm Row, EH7 4AH

(0131) 556 4558

Bus: Lothian 7, 10, 11, 12, 14, 16, 22, 25 ,49, N11, N22, N25   Rail: Waverley

11(12.30 Sun) - 11.45(12.45am Fri & Sat)

Caledonian Deuchars IPA[H] ☺

Late Victorian bar that has been significantly changed. Now brighter and more open plan but still a locals' bar. Very comfy green leather armchairs and bench seating throughout.

OD (pavement tables)   DW

Winston's   N6

20 Kirk Loan, EH12 7HD (off St.Johns Road)

(0131) 539 7077

Bus: Lothian 12, 26, 31, X48, N26, N31

11 - 11.30(Midnight Thu-Sat); 12.30 - 11 Sun

Caledonian Deuchars IPA; 3 Guest Beers[H] ☺

This comfortable lounge bar is situated in Corstorphine, just over a mile from Murrayfield stadium and not far from the zoo. The small, modern building houses a warm and welcoming active community pub. The single room is used by old and young alike. The decor features golfing and rugby themes. The lunchtime meals feature wonderful homemade pies.

OD (pavement Table)   ML (12-2.30)   BS   CW (until 3pm)   DW

Wm Mather & Son   (BS)   T4

25 Broughton Street, EH1 3JU

(0131) 556 6754

Bus: Lothian 1, 4, 5, 7, 8, 10, 11, 12, 14, 15/15A, 16, 17, 19, 22, 25, 26, 34, 44/44A, 45, 49, N3, N8, N11, N16, N22, N25, N26, N37, N44   Rail: Waverley

11 - Midnight(1am Fri & Sat); 12.30 - 11.30 Sun

Caledonian Deuchars IPA, 80; Theakston's Old Peculier; Guest Beer[H] ☺

Convivial split level pub. The lower half has wooden flooring, some fine tiling and woodwork and a good gantry housing an impressive display of cask strength whiskies. Details of food, ales and whisky are displayed on blackboards. The upper level is carpeted and has prints of old Edinburgh. Both levels have a real fire and are well supplied with TVs.

ML (12-3)   BS   DW

Wm McEwans Alehouse   U6

18-22 Clerk Street, EH8 9HX

(0131) 662 6884

Bus: Lothian 3/3A, 5, 7, 8, 14, 29, 30, 31, 33, 37, 47, 49, N3, N8, N30, N31, N37

11(12.30 Sun) - 11(1am Thu-Sat)

Caledonian Deuchars IPA, 80[H]

Modern alehouse with horseshoe counter, celebrating a famous Edinburgh brewing name.

DA

World   E2

55-59 Thistle Street, EH2 1DY

(0131) 225 3275

Bus: City Centre   Rail: Waverley

5 - 1am; Closed Sun & Mon

Caledonian Deuchars IPA[H]

Large wooden floored pub on two levels. At the end of the marble topped bar is an in house Karaoke machine making it lively at weekends.

CW

World's End   K4

2-8 High Street, EH1 1TB

(0131) 556 3628

Bus: Lothian 35, 36 (or 3/3A, 5, 7, 8, 14, 29, 30, 31, 33, 37, 47, X47, X48, 49, N3, N8, N30, N31, N37 to Tron)   Rail: Waverley

11(10 Sat & Sun) - 1am

Belhaven 80/-; Greene King IPA; Greene King Old Speckled Hen; Guest Beer[H] ☺

Busy Old Town lounge bar. On the site of the old Flodden wall dividing Edinburgh from the rest of the world. Some of the original 16c walls are retained. Pictures of traditional Edinburgh scenes and personalities decorate the walls. There is a separate eating area.

ML   MD (11-9 Sat & Sun)   BS

Garvald

Garvald Inn

Garvald, EH41 4LN

(01620) 830311

Bus: Post Bus

12-3, 5-11(Midnight Fri & Sat); 12.30 - 11(5 Winter)
Sun; Closed Mon

Beer Range (1) Varies[H] ☺

Family-run 18th century pub in a pretty village by the
Lammermuir Hills. The bar is cosy and welcoming,
with half-panelled walls, a crimson colour scheme
and a wall with exposed stone. The single real ale is
often from Stewart Brewing or Hadrian & Border.
Popular for food, which is served in both the bar and
tiny dining room. The dinner menu is particularly
impressive. Occasional live music.

*OD (patio) ML (12-2.30) ME (6.30-8.30(9 Fri &
Sat)) BS CW (toys provided) DW*

Gifford

Goblin Ha' Hotel

Main Street, EH41 4QH

(01620) 810244

11 - Midnight(1am Fri & Sat; 11 Sun)

**Caledonian Deuchars IPA, Hop Back Summer
Lightning; 2 Guest Beers[H]** ☺

A long-established inn near the village green. With
colourful decor and light stained wood, the focus is
on food in the smart contemporary lounge bar and
conservatories, though an area is available for
drinking. Non-diners may prefer the more rustic
public bar, with its half wood, half stone walls. A
games room leads off the bar. Live music on 3rd
Friday of each month.

*AC DA (lounge only) OD MD (11-9.30) BS
CW (until 8pm, lounge & conservatory) DW (bar
only)*

Glencorse

Flotterstone Inn

Milton Bridge, EH26 0PP (off A702 by Pentlands
visitor centre)

(01968) 673717

Bus: McEwans 100 (Ed - Dumfries)

11.30(12.30 Sun) - 11

Stewart Pentland IPA; 2 Guest Beers[H] ☺

The large rectangular lounge bar has church pew
seating and numerous Toby jugs and plates around
the walls. A modern timber clad extension overlooks
the enclosed garden and provides additional space.
Good food is served all day in two dining rooms,
which have bare stone walls and wooden ceilings. A
handy place to recover from a day on the Pentland
hills, so can be busy at weekends.

*DA OD MD (12-9(9.30 Fri; 9.30 Sat)) BS CW
DW (bar only, on lead)*

Gorebridge

Stobbs Mill Inn

25 Powdermill Brae, EH23 4HX

(01875) 820202

Bus: Lothian 3/3A, 29(G'bridge)

11(12.30 Sun) - 11(11.30 Thu & Sun; Midnight Fri &
Sat); Closed 3-6 Tue & Thu

Guest Beer[H]

A friendly locals' bar with 3 engraved wooden panels
of sporting scenes which separate it from an
intriguingly tiny snug. Also a lounge, which only
opens when food is served. The guest beer is usually
from a smaller brewery.

*OD (expected Jun08) ML (Sun only) ME (Fri &
Sat only) BS DW*

Gullane

Old Clubhouse

East Links Road, EH31 2AF (W end of village, off
A198)

(01620) 842008

Bus: First 124, X5

11(12.30 Sun) - 11(Midnight Thu-Sat)

**Caledonian Deuchars IPA; Taylor Landlord;
Guest Beer (2 summer); Weston's Cider [P]** ☺

There's a Colonial touch to this pub, which looks out
over the golf links to the Lammermuir Hills. The
half-panelled walls are adorned with historic
memorabilia and stuffed animals. Caricature style
statuettes of the Marx Brothers and Laurel and Hardy
look down from the gantry. Food features highly, the

extensive menu including seafood, pasta, barbecue, curries, salads and burgers.

DA   OD (patio)   MD (12-9.30)   BS   CW (until 8pm)   DW

Haddington

Laffin Duck

1/5 Nungate Bridge, EH41 4BE (by river)

(01620) 825674

Bus: First 6, 44, 6, X6, X8 (High St.)

11(12.30 Sun) - 11(1am Thu & Fri)

Caledonian Deuchars IPA, 80[H]

Gastro pub in a picture postcard setting by the old Nungate Bridge. Formally the Waterside Bistro, it offers various eating areas in addition to the bar with its fine marble topped counter.

OD (garden, patio & tables at front)   MD (12-9)   BS   CW

Tyneside Tavern

10 Poldrate, EH41 4DA

(01620) 822221

Bus: First 6, 44, X6, X8 (High St.)

11(12.30 Sun) - 11(Midnight Thu & Sun; 12.45am Fri & Sat)

Caledonian Deuchars IPA, 80; 2 Guest Beers[H] ☺

Set close to the River Tyne near an old water mill, this community pub has a long narrow bar that attracts a mixed clientele and is popular for watching TV sport. The lounge has been extended and is now a busy bistro at lunchtimes, evenings and all day on Sun. It has wooden floors plus wood-topped tables with cast iron legs. Guest beers are from the S&N guest list.

DA   OD (side close)   ML (12-2.30)   ME (5-9)   MD (12.30-7 Sun)   BS   CW (until 9pm)   DW

Victoria Inn

9 Court Street, EH41 3JD

(01620) 823332

Bus: First 6, 44, X6, X8

11(12.30 Sun) - 11(Midnight Fri & Sat)

Beer Range (2) Varies[H]

A former "local" that has been transformed into a stylish eatery. There's a restaurant, a lounge area and

a cosy bar with circular counter. Though focussed on food, drinkers are welcome.

AC   DA   OD (pavement tables)   ML (12-2)   ME (6-9.30)   MD (12.30-8 Sun)   CW

Ingliston

Turnhouse Bar

Edinburgh Airport, EH12 9DN (upstairs)

(0131) 344 3030

Bus: Lothian 35, Airlink 100, N22; Horsburgh 777; Stagecoach 747

5am(12.30 Sun) - 11

Caledonian Deuchars IPA, 80; Guest Beer[H] ☺

This Wetherspoons bar is a mix of grey and plaid. Half of the fixtures are bar height, with tall stools, some lower banquette seating and tables. Untypical of an airport bar, in that an effort has been made to fit it out as a pub, with a low ceiling and soft lighting. Sadly the view has been spoilt by a multi-story car park.

DA (airport toilets)   MD   BS   CW

Wetherspoons Airside Bar

Edinburgh Airport, EH12 9DN

(0131) 344 3032

Bus: Lothian 35, Airlink 100; N22; Horsburgh 777; Stagecoach 747

4am - Departure of last flight

Caledonian Deuchars IPA, 80[H]

Large bar in departure lounge overlooking the main runway. Access only to air travellers who have passed through security. The smaller Wetherspoons Express has no real ale.

DA   MD (until 21.30)   CW

Juniper Green

Juniper Green Inn

542 Lanark Road, EH14 5EL

(0131) 458 5395

Bus: Lothian 44/44A, 45, N44; Prentice 424

11(12.30 Sun) - 11(Midnight Thu-Sat)

Caledonian Deuchars IPA; 2 Guest Beers[H] ☺

Well appointed, single roomed, lounge bar in late 1800s building. The decor is very clean and attractive throughout, and a very strong community spirit exists within the pub. The bar counter is mahogany and a more modern gantry is designed to match. Pictures of the old Balerno branch line provide interest. The food is freshly cooked to a high standard. Not a pub to visit if you're wearing dirty overalls.

OD (garden & patio) ML

Kinleith Arms

604 Lanark Road,, EH14 5EN

(0131) 453 3214

Bus: Lothian 44/44A, 45, N44; Prentice 424

11(12.30 Sun) - 11(Midnight Thu, 1am Fri & Sat)

Caledonian Deuchars IPA; Guest Beer[H]

Two roomed pub with island bar separating the public bar and larger lounge/eating area.

OD (deck at rear) ML   MD (Wed-Sun) DW (not meal times)

Tanners

459 Lanark Road, EH14 5BA

(0131) 453 3152

Bus: Lothian 44/44A, 45, N44; Prentice 424

11(12.30 Sun) - 11.30(Midnight Wed-Sat)

Caledonian Deuchars IPA, 80; Ocassional Guest Beer[H]

Spacious, lounge bar with restaurant attached. Entry for over 21's only and no work clothes after 7pm.

DA   OD (patio by car park) MD BS CW (if eating)

Kirkliston

Newliston Arms Hotel

78-82 Main Street, EH29 9AB

(0131) 333 3214

Bus: First 38; Waverley 63

11 - 11(Midnight Thu-Sat)

Caledonian Deuchars IPA; Theakston's Best Bitter[H]   ☺

Village pub with an olde world feel given by the mixture of wood panelling, bare stone and brick finishes. The public bar area has an impressive large horseshoe counter and is joined to a carpeted lounge cum eating area. There is also a function room.

DA   OD (garden & patio) ML (12-3) ME (6-9 Mon & Thu-Sat) MD (12-6 Sun) BS CW (until 8pm) DW

Lasswade

Laird and Dog Hotel

5 High Street, EH18 1NA (A768, near river)

(0131) 663 9219

Bus: Lothian 31, N31; First 141

11(12.30 Sun) - 11.30(11.45 Thu; 12.30am Fri & Sat)

Caledonian Deuchars IPA; Guest Beer[H]   ☺

Comfortable village local catering for all tastes, from those who enjoy a quiet drink or meal to music loving pool players. The guest ale is usually from a smaller brewery. The good food menu is supplemented with daily specials and cheaper bar snacks. Pictures and horse brasses decorate the bar areas. There is also a conservatory, an unusual bottle shaped well and a real fire surrounded by arm chairs.

AC DA   OD (paved area by car park) MD (until 9) BS CW (until 8pm) DW (cats also)

Melville Inn

Dobbies Nursery

12(12.30 Sun) - 11

Caledonian Deuchars IPA, 80; Guest Beer[H]

Newly built M&B Vintage Inn adjacent to a garden centre. The large single room is divided into many separate areas, each with different décor and furnishings. Very much an eating pub, with extensive menu and daily specials.

DA   OD (patio) MD (12-10) CW (until 8pm)

Linlithgow

Four Mary's

65-67 High Street, EH49 7ED

(01506) 842171

Bus: First 38 Rail: Linlithgow

11(12.30 Sun) - 11(11.45 Thu-Sat)

Belhaven 80/-, St. Andrews; Caledonian Deuchars IPA; Greene King Abbot; Guest Beer[H]

Comfortable relaxed pub named after four ladies-in-waiting of Mary, Queen of Scots, who was born in nearby Linlithgow Palace. Hosts beer festivals in

May and October when the number of handpumps is increased to eighteen.

ML (12-3) ME (5-9) MD (12.30-9 Sun) CW

Platform 3

1a High Street, EH49 7AB

(01506) 847405

Bus: First 38 Rail: Linlithgow

10.30(12.30 Sun) - Midnight(1am Fri & Sat)

Caledonian Deuchars IPA; Guest Beer[H]

Small, friendly pub on the railway station approach, originally the public bar of the hotel next door. The guest ale rotates on one pump and is from Cairngorm, Stewart or Harviestoun breweries.

West Port Hotel

18-20 West Port, EH49 7AZ

(01506) 847456

Bus: First 38 Rail: Linlithgow

Caledonian Deuchars IPA; Harviestoun Bitter & Twisted[H]

Hotel dating from the 1790's. Katie Weerie's bar is recommended for a relaxing drink, helped by supply of daily papers and welcoming and attentive service.

AC ML (12-2.30) ME (5-9) BS CW

Livingston

Almond Bank   [Liv]

Designer Outlet, EH54 6XA

(01506) 424190

11(12.30 Sun) - 11(1am Thu-Sat)

Caledonian Deuchars IPA; GK Abbot Ale; 3 Guest Beers[H] ☺

Large single roomed modern lounge bar run by J D Wetherspoon in a town centre shopping complex. Stainless steel fencing encloses raised mezzanine areas. The ceiling has curvilinear features. Popular with younger people and can be very busy and overly vibrant at times.

DA OD (patio with tables) MD (9-11) BS CW (until 8pm)

Lothianbridge

Sun Inn

Lothianbridge, EH22 4TR (A7, near Newtongrange)

(0131) 663 2456

Bus: Lothian 29

11(12 Sun) - Midnight

Caledonian Deuchars IPA; Guest Beer [H] ☺

Old inn offering a friendly welcome to both locals and travellers. The bar caters for drinkers and diners and is tastefully decorated throughout. Local art and a suspended model railway system provide interest. An additional dining area overlooks the garden.

AC OD MD (12-9) BS CW DW

Lothianburn

Steading

118 - 120 Biggar Road, EH10 7DU

(0131) 445 1128

Bus: Lothian 4, 15/15A

11(12.30 Sun) - Midnight(earlier if quiet)

Caledonian Deuchars IPA; Orkney Dark Island; Taylor Landlord; Guest Beer[H] ☺

The pub was converted from farm cottages and has distinct areas for drinkers and diners. The popular restaurant includes a large conservatory extension. Only a simple menu is available in the bar. The outside drinking area has excellent views of the Pentland Hills and the pub is ideally placed for a relaxing pint after walking in the hills or visiting the nearby dry ski-slope.

OD MD BS CW DW

Mid Calder

Black Bull

Market Street, EH53 0AA

(01506) 882170

Bus: First 27, 28, X25, X27, X28, 427; Horsburgh 777; Prentice 400, 401

11(12.30 Sun) - 11(Midnight Fri & Sat)

Caledonian Deuchars IPA; Guest Beer[H]

Fine old public bar with wooden interior. Also a comfortable open plan lounge which is popular for food. Both are decorated with country photos and prints. The guest beers are chosen by customers. The bar may only be open in the evening.

OD (walled garden)   MD (12(12.30 Sun)-8.45)   BS   CW (until 8pm, lounge only)   DW (not lounge)

Milton Bridge

Countryside

Roslin Road South, EH26 0NZ (by Auchendinny on map)

(01968) 676884

Bus: Lothian 15/15A, 37, 47, X47, N37

12(12.30 Sun) - 9

Caledonian Deuchars IPA[H]

Plush, wood panelled, lounge bar with a conservatory extension. Very food orientated, hence the unusual closing time. However, the bar has plenty of tables for those not seeking food.

DA   OD (picnic benches)   MD   CW

Musselburgh

Levenhall Arms

10 Ravensheugh Road, EH21 7PP

(0131) 665 3220

Bus: Lothian 15/15A, 26, N26   Rail: Wallyford

12(12.30 Sun) - 11(Midnight Thu & Sun; 1am Fri & Sat)

Stewart Pentland IPA; Guest Beer[H]   ☺

This three roomed hostelry dates from 1830 and is popular with locals and race-goers. The lively, cheerfully decorated public bar is half-timber panelled and carpeted. A smaller area leads off, with a darts board and pictures of old local industries. The quieter lounge area, with vinyl banquettes, is used for food. Opening times and menu may vary in winter.

MD (12-8; limited in winter)   BS   CW (until 8.30, in lounge)   DW (bar only)

Volunteer Arms (Staggs)

81 North High Street, EH21 6JE (behind Brunton Hall)

(0131) 665 9654

Bus: Lothian 15/15A, 26, 30, 44/44A, N44; First 141

12 - 11(11.30 Thu; Midnight Fri & Sat); 1 - 10 Sun

Caledonian Deuchars IPA; 3 Guest Beers[H]   ☺

Superb pub run by the same family since 1858. The bar and snug are traditional with a wooden floor, wood panelling and mirrors from defunct local breweries. The splendid gantry is topped with old casks. The snug has a nascent history collection about local breweries. The more modern lounge opens at the weekend. The three guest beers, often pale and hoppy, change very regularly. CAMRA Lothian pub of the year 2008.

OD   DW (bar only)

Newcraighall

Cuddie Brae   Y5

91 Newcraighall Road, EH21 8SG

(0131) 657 1212

Bus: Lothian 30, N30   Rail: Newcraighall

11(12.30 Sun) - 11

Beer Range (2) Varies[H]   ☺

This modern pub aspires to an olde worlde feel with exposed brickwork, wooden beams and numerous knick-knacks. It is broken into several areas for drinking and eating, which are comfortably furnished. A budget hotel and a fitness centre are next door and the Newcraighall shopping complex is just down the road.

DA   OD (patio)   MD (11(12.30 Sun)-10)   BS   CW (until 10pm)

Volunteer Arma (Staggs)
CAMRA 2008 Lothian Pub of the Year and past winner of CAMRA National Pub of the Year

North Berwick

Auld Hoose

19 Forth Street, EH39 4HX

(01620) 892692

Bus: First 124, X5   Rail: N. Berwick

11 - 11(1am Thu-Sat); 12.30 - Midnight Sun

Beer Range (2) Varies[H]   ☺

Interesting high ceilinged traditional pub with half stone and half wood panelled walls, plus wooden floor. The three-bay gantry has carved pillars and supports six old whisky casks. The L shaped lounge has a more modern appearance.

DA   BS   CW (until 7.30, in lounge)   DW

County Hotel

17 High Street, EH39 4HH

Bus: First 124, X5   Rail: N. Berwick

11 - 11(1am Fri & Sat)

Guest Beer[H]

The only relatively untouched pub in the town. A low ceiling and narrow half-wood panelled walls give it a cosy feel, especially in winter when the coal fire is burning. Prints of old N. Berwick life adorn the walls.

AC (17 en-suite rooms)   DA   OD (garden)   MD (12-9)   BS   CW (until 8pm)   DW

E. Lothian Yacht Club

Harbour

(01620) 892698

Bus: First 124, X5   Rail: N. Berwick

Caledonian Deuchars IPA(summer)[H]

Pleasant bar, with wood beams, in the loft of the clubhouse. WARNING: Entry may be restricted to members.

Golfers Rest

109 High Street, EH39 4HD

(01620) 892320

Bus: First 124, X5   Rail: N. Berwick

11 - 11(1am Thu-Sat); 12.30 - Midnight Sun

Caledonian Deuchars IPA ☺

A community pub, this spacious lounge bar hosts a Friday poker league, a quiz night, live entertainment on Sat. evening along with pool and darts. TV sport is also popular.

DA   ML (12-2.30; not Sun)   BS   CW (until 7pm) DW (on a lead)

Nether Abbey Hotel

20 Dirleton Avenue, EH39 4BQ (A198, 3/4 mile W of centre)

(01620) 892802

Bus: First 124, X5   Rail: N. Berwick

11 - 11(Midnight Thu; 1am Fri & Sat)

Beer Range (4) Varies[A] ☺

Family run hotel in a stone built villa offering a bright, contemporary interior comprising one open plan, split level room. The lower area is a bar and the upper a restaurant. The marble topped bar counter has a row of modern chrome founts. The middle ones, with horizontally moving levers, dispense the real ales.

AC   DA   OD (front patio)   ML (12-2.30)   ME (6-9) MD (summer & Fri-Sun)   BS   CW (until 9pm)   DW

Ship

7/9 Quality Street, EH39 4HJ

(01620) 890676

Bus: First 124, X5   Rail: N. Berwick

11 - 11(Midnight Thu-Sat)

Caledonian Deuchars IPA; 2 Guest Beers[A] ☺

Open plan bar, split into three areas by a glass partition and a twice pierced wall. It has pine floorboards, a mahogany counter and a dark stained wooden gantry. Real ale is dispensed from founts, which look similar to those dispensing the keg beers so look carefully at the pump clips. Popular for food. Live music regularly on Saturday nights.

OD (pavement tables & patio)   ML (12-3(4 weekends))   BS   CW (until 8pm)   DW

Pathhead

Stair Arms Hotel

PATHHEAD, EH37 5TX (on A68, 1/2m north of village)

(01875) 320277

Bus: Munro 20

11(12 Sun) - 11(1am Fri & Sat)

Guest Ale[H] ☺

In 1841 a farm steading was converted into a coaching inn, a reminder of which stands outside. Now extended into an elegant road side hotel with comfortable lounge areas. Adjoining the bar is a dining room with lath and plaster effect walls, wooden ceiling beams and an impressive fireplace. Hidden to the rear are TV and function rooms. The restaurant has a real fire and the menu features Scottish food.

AC   DA   OD (garden)   MD (12(12.30 Sun)-9(9.30 Fri & Sat))   BS   CW   DW (bar only)

Pencaitland

Winton Arms

Main Street, EH34 5DN

(01875) 341278

Bus: Lothian 44 (eve & Sun); First 44B, X13

2.30 - 11.30(Midnight Thu); 1 - 1am Fri; 12 - 1am Sat; 12 - Midnight Sun

Caledonian 80; Guest Beer[H] ☺

Refurbished to give a brighter feel, the bar has a wood effect floor, bare stone walls and artexed ceiling. The lounge is similar but with a carpet. Old pictures of Pencaitland and environs adorn the walls, and a fine selection of sporting trophies present a glittering roof to the gents!

DA   OD   BS   DW

Penicuik

Navaar

23 Bog Road, EH26 9BY (just W of centre)

(01968) 672693

Bus: Lothian 37, X47, 15, 47, N37: First 141

12 - 1am(Midnight Sun)

Stewart Pentland IPA[H] ☺

A lively pub with a strong community spirit, situated in an old private house, circa 1870. The large bar is open plan with a log/coal fire and TV screens. There is also a restaurant, with an extensive a la carte menu. Snacks are available in the bar.

AC   OD (garden & patio)   MD   BS   DW

Prestonpans

Prestoungrange Gothenburg

227 High St., EH32 9BE

(01875) 819922

Bus: Lothian 26, N26

11(12.30 Sun) - 11(1am Fri & Sat)

Beer Range (2) Varies[A] ☺

Superbly re-furbished Gothenburg pub. Winner of the 2005 English Heritage pub refurbishment award and on CAMRA's National Pub Inventory. The magnificent painted ceiling in the bar has to be seen to be appreciated and there is also a bistro. Upstairs is a lounge and function room with superb views over the Forth. The walls throughout are covered in murals and paintings depicting past local life. Fowler's micro-brewery is currently out of action.

DA   ML (12.30-2.30)   ME (5.30-8.30)   MD (12.30-9 Fri & Sat(7.30 Sun))   BS   CW

Ratho

Bridge Inn

27 Baird Road, EH28 8RA (by canal)

(0131) 333 1320

Bus: Lothian X48 (Ratho)

11.30(12.30 Sun) - 11(Midnight Fri & Sat)

Caledonian Deuchars IPA; Stewart Pentland IPA; Guest Beer (Summer)[H] ☺

Food orientated old canal side inn. The older part, originally a farmhouse dating from around 1750 and predating the canal, is used as a restaurant. A modern extension is a lounge bar cum dining area with views over the canal. The inn was a focal point during the long campaign to restore the canal, part of the Millennium Link project. Cruises can be pre-booked in the restaurant barge throughout the year.

DA   OD   MD (10-9.30)   BS   CW (if well behaved)

Roslin

Roslin Glen Hotel

2 Penicuik Road, EH25 9LH

(0131) 440 2029

Bus: Lothian 15; First 141

11 - 11

Stewart Pentland IPA[H]

Hotel with a strong emphasis on food. The well appointed lounge bar is adorned with pictures, many of nearby Rosslyn Chapel. The more functional public bar has a pool table. Real ale only in lounge, but can be ordered in the bar.

AC   MD (12-8.45(9.15 Fri & Sat))   BS   CW (in lounge)   DW (bar only)

South Queensferry

Anchor Inn

10 Edinburgh Road, EH30 9HR

(0131) 331 3684

Bus: First 43   Rail: Dalmeny

11 - 11.30(1am Fri & Sat); 12.30 - 11 Sun

Caledonian Deuchars IPA[P] ☺

Busy, small, single roomed, comfortable, locals' bar in a building dating from 1886 located in the historic village centre. Banquette seating surrounds the room. A high shelf is adorned with sporting trophies. The Deuchars is real even though it is served in a similar way to the keg beers.

BS

Ferry Tap

36 High Street, EH30 9HN

(0131) 331 2000

Bus: First 43   Rail: Dalmeny

11(12.30 Sun) - 11.30(Midnight Thu; 12.30am Fri & Sat)

Caledonian Deuchars IPA, 80; Orkney Dark Island; Stewart 80/-; Guest Beer[H]

One-roomed L-shaped bar with an unusual barrel-vaulted ceiling. Dark wood gives an intimate feel and numerous artefacts, many from bygone breweries, add interest. A good selection of meals are served. WARNING: Ownership changed in Apr 08.

ML (12-3; 12.30-6 Sun)   ME (5-8 Mon-Sat)   CW   DW

Hawes Inn

7 Newhalls Road, EH30 9TA

(0131) 331 1990

Bus: First 43   Rail: Dalmeny

11 - 11; 12.30 - 10.30 Sun

Caledonian Deuchars IPA; Taylor Landlord; 2 Guest Beers[H] ☺

Old coaching inn by the river over-shadowed by the mighty Forth bridge. Modernised, despite local objections, a few years ago into a multi-roomed pub with salvaged furniture and wooden beams creating an "olde worlde" feel. Very food orientated, but with an internal bar area to the rear. Featured in the writings of Robert Louis Stevenson.

AC   DA   OD   MD (12-10(12.30-9.30 Sun))   BS   CW

Orocco Pier

17 High Street, EH30 9PP

(0131) 331 1298

Bus: First 43   Rail: Dalmeny

11 - 1am

Caledonian Deuchars IPA[P]

Classy upmarket hotel with stylish and contemporary décor. Renowned for its fine dining in a choice of bar areas. Great views of the bridges from the rear deck.

AC   OD (deck overlooking Forth)   MD

Uphall

Oatridge Hotel

2-4 East Main Street, EH52 5DA

(01506) 856465

11(12.30 Sun) - Midnight

Beer Range (3) Varies[H]

Originally a 19th century coaching inn. Real ale is served in the public bar, which has a stylish art deco feel and displays a collection of ceramic vessels that originally held refreshing liquids. There is also a large etched mirror depicting scenes of yesteryear. TV sport is popular at the weekend, and pool is also played.

AC OD   MD

CAMPAIGN FOR REAL ALE

Application to join CAMRA

I/We wish to join the Campaign for Real Ale and agree to abide by the Memorandum and Articles of Association.

Your details

Title ……………….. Surname ……………………………………………………......

Forename(s) ……………………………………………………………......………………..

Address ……………………………………………………..……………..…..

……………….....……………………………………………..…………………….

………………………………………… Postcode……………………..…

Telephone ……………………………………...…………….home / work / mob

Email …………………………………………………………………………..

Your partner's details (if joint membership)

Title ……………….. Surname ………………………...……..............………....

Forename(s) …………………………………......……..………………………….

Please send this form and a cheque payable to CAMRA for £22 for Single Membership (UK & EU) or £27 for Joint Membership (UK & EU at the same address) to: the Membership Secretary, CAMRA, 230 Hatfield Road, St. Albans, Herts., AL1 4BR. For concessionary, life membership and overseas rates or for Direct Debit payment visit www.camra.org.uk or call **01727 867201.**

Signed …………………………….……………………………………….

Date ………………………….....